Sweet Old-fashioned FAVOURITES

Of all the tastes we remember with the most intense pleasure and nostalgia, those sweet old-fashioned favourites of childhood usually head the list. We have gathered together around 160 of our most well-known and best loved pastries, cakes, puddings, biscuits and other sweet treats. Many have a long history going back hundreds of years. Others are comparative youngsters, created by cake shops in the last 30 or 40 years. For easy reference, we have listed recipes by their most commonly used name, in alphabetical order. We have also included some tips to help you achieve the best results, along with some of the more interesting historical snippets we discovered. If you are not familiar with any of the ingredients, please refer to the glossary on page 123. Most of these recipes involve baking, so it is important to follow instructions carefully for perfect results. You will find a picture of most of the bakeware we used on page 125.

Pamela Clark

EDITORIAL & FOOD DIRECTOR

BRITISH AND NORTH AMERICAN READERS:
Please note that Australian cup and spoon measurements are metric. A quick conversion guide appears on page 126. A glossary explaining unfamiliar terms and ingredients appears on page 123.

Afghan Biscuits

180g butter
⅓ cup caster sugar
1½ cups plain flour
1 tablespoon cocoa
1 cup Corn Flakes, lightly crushed
¼ cup coconut, toasted

CHOCOLATE ICING
¾ cup icing sugar
1 tablespoon cocoa
1 teaspoon soft butter
2 tablespoons water, approximately

Beat butter and sugar in small bowl with electric mixer until light and fluffy. Stir in sifted flour and cocoa, then Corn Flakes and coconut in 2 batches. Place 3 level teaspoons of mixture together about 3cm apart on lightly greased oven trays.

Bake in moderate oven about 12 minutes or until biscuits are firm and lightly browned. Stand biscuits 5 minutes before lifting onto wire rack to cool. Spread warm chocolate icing quickly onto biscuits.
Chocolate Icing: Combine sifted icing sugar and cocoa in small heatproof bowl, stir in butter and enough water to make a stiff paste. Stir over hot water until spreadable.
Makes about 30.
■ Biscuits can be made a week ahead.
■ Storage: Airtight container.
■ Freeze: Uniced biscuits suitable.
■ Microwave: Not suitable.

Anzac Biscuits

It is known that variations of Scottish oatmeal biscuits were made at home and sent to soldiers of the Australian and New Zealand Army Corps (ANZAC) in World War I. However, the Australian War Memorial, Canberra, ACT, suggests that they were not named Anzac Biscuits until after World War I, when they were made and sold as fund-raisers for returned soldiers.

It is best to use the traditional (not quick cook) oats in our version.
1 cup rolled oats
1 cup plain flour
1 cup sugar
¾ cup coconut
125g butter
1 tablespoon golden syrup
1 teaspoon bicarbonate of soda
2 tablespoons boiling water

Combine oats, sifted flour, sugar and coconut in large bowl. Combine butter and golden syrup in pan, stir over low heat until butter is melted. Combine soda and water, add to butter mixture, stir into dry ingredients while mixture is warm.

Place 3 level teaspoons of mixture together about 4cm apart on greased oven trays, press down lightly. Bake in slow oven about 20 minutes or until golden brown. Loosen biscuits while warm, cool on trays.
Makes about 30.
■ Recipe can be made 4 days ahead.
■ Storage: Airtight container.
■ Freeze: Suitable.
■ Microwave: Not suitable.

RIGHT: From left: Afghan Biscuits, Anzac Biscuits.

Tea set and square plate from Villeroy & Boch; blue-rimmed plate from Victoria and Francesca, Woollahra Antiques Centre; lace serviette from Appley Hoare Antiques; table from Country Form.

Apple Brown Betty

Originally made with apples, suet and breadcrumbs, this was a popular pudding with poorer country people in 19th century Britain. Ours, without suet, is a treat with sweet lemon flavouring.

Any favourite stewed fruit can be substituted for apples.

2 cups (140g) stale breadcrumbs
3 large (about 750g) apples
1 teaspoon grated lemon rind

LEMON SYRUP
½ cup golden syrup
¼ cup water
½ cup sugar
¼ cup lemon juice

Grease shallow ovenproof dish (6 cup capacity), sprinkle with a layer of breadcrumbs. Peel, core and grate apples coarsely, combine with rind in bowl.

Spread a layer of apple mixture over breadcrumbs. Repeat layering, finishing with breadcrumbs.

Pour hot lemon syrup evenly over apple and bread mixture. Bake, uncovered, in slow oven about 1¼ hours or until lightly browned. Serve warm with cream, custard or ice-cream.
Lemon Syrup: Combine golden syrup, water and sugar in pan, stir over heat, without boiling, until sugar is dissolved, remove from heat; stir in juice.
Serves 4.

- ■ Recipe can be made a day ahead.
- ■ Storage: Covered, in refrigerator.
- ■ Freeze: Not suitable.
- ■ Microwave: Not suitable.

BELOW: Apple Brown Betty.
RIGHT: Apple Cake.

Below: China from Waterford Wedgwood; silver spoon from Woollahra Cottage, Woollahra Antiques Centre; tablecloth from Aginian's; table from Country Form. Right: China from Royal Doulton; table from Victoria and Francesca, Woollahra Antiques Centre.

Apple Cake

Apples are baked on top of a melt-in-the-mouth butter cake, then glazed with apricot jam. The cake can be served warm as a dessert with whipped cream.

180g butter
2 teaspoons grated lemon rind
⅔ cup caster sugar
3 eggs
1 cup self-raising flour
½ cup plain flour
⅓ cup milk
2 medium (about 300g) apples
2 teaspoons water
1 teaspoon gelatine
2 tablespoons apricot jam, strained

Grease 20cm springform tin or deep 20cm round cake pan, cover base with paper, grease paper.

Beat butter, rind and sugar in small bowl with electric mixer until light and fluffy. Beat in eggs 1 at a time, beat until combined. Transfer mixture to large bowl, stir in sifted flours and milk, spread into prepared pan.

Peel, quarter and core apples. Make lengthways cuts into rounded sides of apple quarters, cutting about three-quarters of the way through. Place quarters, rounded side up, around edge of cake. Bake cake in moderate oven about 1 hour or until browned. Stand 5 minutes before turning onto wire rack.

Heat water in pan, sprinkle over gelatine, stir, without boiling, until gelatine is dissolved, remove from heat, stir in jam. Brush jam mixture over top of hot cake; cool before cutting.

■ Recipe can be made a day ahead.
■ Storage: Airtight container.
■ Freeze: Not suitable.
■ Microwave: Not suitable.

Apple Charlotte

The many different types of charlotte include French, English and Australian versions. A lovely legend is that the classic charlotte was named after Charlotte, heroine of Goethe's romance, "The Sorrows of Young Werther", published in 1774. However, ours is the popular Australian version; it is similar to an apple pie, and has rich pastry with passionfruit icing.

1⅓ cups plain flour
1 cup self-raising flour
⅓ cup custard powder
⅓ cup cornflour
2 tablespoons icing sugar
150g butter
⅓ cup water, approximately
milk

FILLING
6 medium (about 1kg) apples
2 tablespoons sugar
¼ cup water
1 tablespoon lemon juice
½ teaspoon ground nutmeg

PASSIONFRUIT ICING
1 cup icing sugar
½ teaspoon soft butter
1 passionfruit
1 teaspoon milk, approximately

Grease 20cm round sandwich pan. Sift dry ingredients into large bowl, rub in butter. Add enough water to make ingredients cling together. Press dough into ball, knead gently on floured surface until smooth, cover, refrigerate 30 minutes.

Roll two-thirds of the dough on lightly floured surface until large enough to line base and side of prepared pan. Lift pastry into pan, brush edge of pastry with a little milk. Spread cold filling into pastry case.

Roll remaining pastry until large enough to cover filling, place pastry over filling, press edges together, trim edges. Brush pastry with a little more milk, cut 2 slits in pastry. Bake in moderate oven about 50 minutes or until lightly browned. Cool charlotte in pan before turning out.

Top cold charlotte with passionfruit icing, leave to set before cutting.

Filling: Peel, quarter, core and thinly slice apples. Combine apples, sugar, water, juice and nutmeg in pan, bring to boil, cover, simmer about 10 minutes or until apples are tender, drain, cool.

Passionfruit Icing: Sift icing sugar into small heatproof bowl, stir in butter, passionfruit pulp and enough milk to make a stiff paste. Stir icing over hot water, until spreadable.

Serves 6 to 8.
- Recipe can be made a day ahead.
- Storage: Covered, in refrigerator.
- Freeze: Not suitable.
- Microwave: Filling suitable.

BELOW: Apple Charlotte.
RIGHT: From left: Apple Pie, Apple Crumble.

Below: China from Waterford Wedgwood; knife from Woollahra Cottage, Woollahra Antiques Centre; tablecloth from Aginian's. Right: Blue and white bowl and jug from Accoutrement; bowl with apples, flour sifter and table from Country Form.

Apple Crumble

Tender apple chunks are a tempting contrast to the crisp spice and brown sugar topping.

Try a combination of stewed apple and rhubarb, or apricots or berries; they are all good.

5 large (about 1¼kg) apples
¼ cup sugar
¼ cup water
CRUMBLE
¾ cup self-raising flour
½ teaspoon ground cinnamon
80g butter
½ cup brown sugar, firmly packed

Grease ovenproof dish (5 cup capacity). Peel, core and cut apples into eighths. Combine apples, sugar and water in large pan, cover, cook over low heat about 10 minutes or until apples are tender. Drain apples, spread into prepared dish, sprinkle evenly with crumble mixture. Bake in moderate oven about 30 minutes or until lightly browned.

Crumble: Combine sifted flour and cinnamon in bowl, rub in butter, add sugar, mix well.

Serves 4 to 6.

■ Recipe can be made 2 hours before serving.
■ Storage: Covered, in refrigerator.
■ Freeze: Not suitable.
■ Microwave: Apples suitable.

Apple Pie

Granny Smith apples, with their green skins and crisp, sweet flesh, are ideal for this pie. They were named after Maria Anne Smith, wife of Thomas Smith, of Eastwood, Sydney, NSW. She cultivated this variety from Tasmanian apple seeds.

1 cup plain flour
½ cup self-raising flour
¼ cup cornflour
¼ cup custard powder
1 tablespoon caster sugar
100g butter
1 egg, separated
⅓ cup water, approximately
1 tablespoon caster sugar, extra

APPLE FILLING
10 medium (about 1½kg) apples
½ cup water
2 tablespoons sugar
¼ teaspoon ground cinnamon
1 teaspoon grated lemon rind

Sift flours, custard powder and sugar into bowl, rub in butter. Add egg yolk and enough water to make ingredients cling together. Press dough into ball, knead lightly on floured surface until smooth, cover, refrigerate 30 minutes. Divide dough in half. Roll 1 portion between sheets of greaseproof paper until large enough to line base and side of 23cm pie plate. Lift pastry into pie plate. Spoon cold apple filling into pastry case, brush edge of pastry with lightly beaten egg white.

Roll remaining pastry large enough to cover filling, place pastry over filling.

Press edges together, trim, pinch edges decoratively. Decorate with pastry scraps, if desired. Brush pastry with a little more egg white. Sprinkle with extra sugar.

Bake in hot oven 20 minutes, reduce heat to moderate, bake about further 25 minutes or until pastry is well browned.

Apple Filling: Peel, quarter, core and slice apples. Combine apples in large pan with water, cover, simmer about 5 minutes or until apples are tender. Drain apples, discard liquid. Transfer apples to large bowl, gently stir in sugar, cinnamon and rind; cool.

Serves 6 to 8.

■ Recipe can be made a day ahead.
■ Storage: Covered, in refrigerator.
■ Freeze: Not suitable.
■ Microwave: Apples suitable.

Apple Sponge

It is important to have the apple mixture as hot as possible before topping with the sponge mixture. The heat from the apples starts the cooking process.

4 large (about 800g) apples
¼ cup caster sugar
¼ cup water

SPONGE TOPPING
2 eggs
⅓ cup caster sugar
2 tablespoons cornflour
2 tablespoons plain flour
2 tablespoons self-raising flour

Peel, core, quarter and slice apples, combine in pan with sugar and water, cover, cook about 10 minutes or until apples are tender. Spoon hot apple mixture into deep 14cm round ovenproof dish (6 cup capacity) spread with topping. Bake in moderate oven about 25 minutes.

Sponge Topping: Beat eggs in small bowl with electric mixer about 7 minutes or until thick and creamy. Add sugar gradually, beat until dissolved between additions. Fold in sifted flours.
Serves 4 to 6.

■ Recipe best made just before serving.
■ Freeze: Not suitable.
■ Microwave: Apples suitable.

Apple Strudel

In German, the word strudel means eddy or whirlwind, giving an idea of this recipe where thin pastry is wrapped around a filling. Usually considered German or Austrian in origin, the strudel is also claimed by Hungary, where it is called retes; it probably came to all these areas from Turkey, via Yugoslavia, as baklava.

There are many different strudels; ours is an easy version using fillo pastry instead of the traditional strudel dough. Strudel dough is wonderful but takes time and skill to make perfectly.

5 large (about 1kg) apples
¼ cup water
1 teaspoon grated lemon rind
1 clove
½ teaspoon ground cinnamon
½ teaspoon ground nutmeg
2 tablespoons packaged ground almonds
¾ cup walnuts, chopped
¾ cup sultanas
5 sheets fillo pastry
60g butter, melted
2 tablespoons packaged ground almonds, extra
icing sugar

Peel, core, quarter and thinly slice apples, combine in pan with water, rind and clove, cover, cook about 10 minutes or until apples are tender, discard clove, cool.

Combine cold apple mixture in bowl with spices, nuts and sultanas. Layer pastry sheets together, brushing each with butter and sprinkling with extra ground almonds.

Spread filling to within 2cm from the edge of 1 long side, leaving 5cm at each end. Fold ends in, roll up as for Swiss roll. Place strudel on greased oven tray, brush with butter. Bake in moderate oven about 40 minutes or until lightly browned. Dust with sifted icing sugar before serving. Serve warm or cold with custard or cream.
Serves 6.

■ Recipe can be made a day ahead.
■ Storage: Covered, in refrigerator.
■ Freeze: Not suitable.
■ Microwave: Apples suitable.

LEFT: From left: Apple Strudel, Apple Sponge.
ABOVE: Armenian Nutmeg Cake.

Left: China from Villeroy & Boch; cloth from Aginian's; table from Victoria and Francesca, Woollahra Antiques Centre. Above: China from Waterford Wedgwood; napkin from Butler and Co; table from Country Form.

Armenian Nutmeg Cake

Armenian cooking is noted for its flavours and its use of spices. In this recipe, nutmeg adds fragrance and taste to a not-too-sweet cake that cooks in 2 layers; it is very popular with children.

1 cup self-raising flour
1 cup plain flour
1 teaspoon ground nutmeg
125g butter
1½ cups brown sugar, lightly packed
1 teaspoon bicarbonate of soda
¾ cup milk
1 egg, lightly beaten
½ cup chopped walnuts or pecans

Grease 20cm x 30cm lamington pan. Sift flours and nutmeg into large bowl, rub in butter, mix in sugar (or process these ingredients until crumbly). Press 1½ cups of this mixture into prepared pan.

Stir combined soda and milk into remaining dry ingredients with egg and nuts, mix well, pour into prepared pan. Bake in moderate oven about 35 minutes. Stand 5 minutes before turning onto wire rack to cool.

■ Recipe can be made 2 days ahead.
■ Storage: Airtight container.
■ Freeze: Suitable.
■ Microwave: Not suitable.

Baked Apples

Granny Smith apples and Golden Delicious apples are the best varieties to use for baking.

4 medium (about 600g) apples
50g butter, softened
⅓ cup brown sugar
½ cup sultanas
1 teaspoon ground cinnamon

Remove cores from apples, cut 1cm from base of each core, push back into base of each apple to act as a plug. Slit skin of each apple around the centre.

Beat butter and sugar in small bowl until smooth, stir in sultanas and cinnamon. Fill apple cavities with creamed sugar mixture, stand apples in greased ovenproof dish. Bake, uncovered, in moderate oven about 45 minutes or until apples are tender, brush occasionally with pan syrup during cooking.
Serves 4.

▧ Recipe is best made just before serving.
▧ Freeze: Not suitable.
▧ Microwave: Suitable.

Baked Custard

Avoid whisking the eggs too much or the custard will be aerated. The texture of the cooked custard should be creamy smooth but set. Serve hot or cold with stewed or canned fruit and cream, if desired.

6 eggs
2 teaspoons vanilla essence
⅓ cup caster sugar
1 litre (4 cups) hot milk
ground nutmeg

Whisk eggs, essence and sugar together in bowl. Gradually whisk milk into egg mixture, pour into lightly greased ovenproof dish (6 cup capacity), sprinkle with nutmeg. Place in baking dish with enough boiling water to come halfway up side of ovenproof dish. Bake, uncovered in moderate oven about 45 minutes or until custard is firm.
Serves 6.

▧ Recipe can be made a day ahead.
▧ Storage: Covered, in refrigerator.
▧ Freeze: Not suitable.
▧ Microwave: Not suitable.

Bakewell Tart

The name comes from Bakewell Pudding, a popular Derbyshire, UK, pudding; this probably had its origins in Elizabethan times, but was made famous by a cook at the Rutland Arms in Bakewell around 200 years ago. Jane Austen is said to have stayed there while writing "Pride and Prejudice".

100g butter
2 tablespoons caster sugar
1 egg yolk
1 cup plain flour
½ cup packaged ground almonds
1½ tablespoons raspberry jam
2 tablespoons apricot jam

FILLING
125g butter
½ cup caster sugar
2 eggs
¾ cup packaged ground almonds
2 tablespoons rice flour
½ teaspoon grated lemon rind

LEMON ICING
⅓ cup icing sugar
2 teaspoons lemon juice

Cream butter, sugar and egg yolk in small bowl with electric mixer until combined. Stir in sifted flour and almonds in 2 batches. Knead on lightly floured surface until smooth; cover, refrigerate for 30 minutes.

Roll dough between sheets of greaseproof paper until large enough to line 24cm flan tin. Lift pastry into tin, ease into side, trim edges. Spread base of pastry with raspberry jam. Spread filling over jam, place tart on oven tray, bake in moderately hot oven about 25 minutes or until lightly browned.

Place apricot jam in small pan, heat, strain. Brush top of hot tart with hot jam; cool. Pipe or drizzle with lemon icing.
Filling: Cream butter and sugar in small bowl with electric mixer until mixture is light and fluffy, beat in eggs 1 at a time. Stir in almonds, rice flour and rind.
Lemon Icing: Sift icing sugar into small bowl, stir in juice; stir until smooth.
Serves 8.

▧ Recipe can be made a day ahead.
▧ Storage: Airtight container.
▧ Freeze: Suitable.
▧ Microwave: Jam suitable.

LEFT: From left: Baked Apples, Baked Custard.
RIGHT: Bakewell Tart.

Left: Cloth from Accoutrement; tiles from Country Floors.

Banana Fritters

There have been fritters since Roman days; they can be sweet or savoury. The name is probably an adaptation of old English and French words for frying.

Be careful not to over-heat the oil or the fritters will be too brown.

½ cup plain flour
½ cup self-raising flour
1 tablespoon caster sugar
2 eggs, lightly beaten
½ cup milk
1 teaspoon oil
1 teaspoon vanilla essence
4 large bananas, halved
oil for deep-frying
sugar

Sift flours and caster sugar into bowl, gradually whisk in eggs, milk, oil and essence. Dip banana pieces into batter, deep-fry in hot oil until lightly browned; drain on absorbent paper, toss in sugar. Serves 4.
■ Recipe best made just before serving.
■ Freeze: Not suitable.
■ Microwave: Not suitable.

BELOW: Banana Fritters.
RIGHT: Baps.
FAR RIGHT: Berlin Doughnuts.

Baps

Traditional Scottish breakfast rolls, these are very soft and light. They are best eaten hot from the oven.

2 x 7g sachets granulated yeast
2 teaspoons caster sugar
⅔ cup warm water
⅔ cup warm milk
3⅓ cups plain flour
1 teaspoon salt
60g lard

Combine yeast, sugar, water and milk in bowl, cover, stand in warm place about 10 minutes or until mixture is frothy.

Sift flour and salt into large bowl, rub in lard. Stir in yeast mixture, mix to a soft dough, cover, stand in warm place about 1 hour or until dough is doubled in size.

Turn dough onto lightly floured surface, knead about 5 minutes or until smooth. Divide dough into 8 pieces, knead into balls; place baps 5cm apart onto floured oven trays. Dust lightly with a little more sifted flour, cover with a tea-towel. Stand in warm place about 10 minutes or until baps are well risen.

Dust baps again with a little sifted flour. Make an impression in centre of each bap with finger. Bake in hot oven about 15 minutes or until lightly browned. Serve hot with butter.
Makes 8.
■ Recipe best made just before serving.
■ Freeze: Uncooked baps suitable.
■ Microwave: Not suitable.

Berlin Doughnuts

Jelly (or jam) doughnuts are known in Berlin as pfannkuchen and elsewhere in Germany as oder krapfen; they are also sometimes called Bismarcks because the Prussian statesman Bismarck was reputed to be so fond of them.

2 x 7g sachets granulated yeast
¼ cup warm water
1 cup warm milk
¼ cup caster sugar
60g butter, melted
2 eggs, lightly beaten
3¾ cups plain flour
1 teaspoon grated lemon rind
1 egg white, lightly beaten
½ cup raspberry jam, approximately
oil for deep-drying
caster sugar, extra

Combine yeast, water, milk and sugar in small bowl, cover, stand in warm place about 10 minutes or until mixture is frothy.

Stir butter and eggs into yeast mixture. Sift flour into large bowl, stir in yeast mixture and rind, mix to a soft dough. Cover, stand in warm place about 45 minutes or until dough is doubled in size.

Turn dough onto lightly floured surface, knead dough about 5 minutes or until smooth. Roll dough about 5 minutes or until smooth. Roll dough until about 1cm thick; cut into 5cm rounds.

Brush half the rounds with egg white, drop about 1 teaspoon of jam in centre of each round; top with remaining rounds, pinch edges together. Re-roll remaining dough, cut into rounds, repeat with remaining egg white and jam. Loosely cover rounds with oiled plastic wrap, stand in warm place about 10 minutes, or until almost doubled in size.

Deep-fry doughnuts in batches in hot oil until well browned, turning once. Drain on absorbent paper, toss doughnuts immediately in extra sugar.
Makes about 25.
■ Recipe can be made a day ahead.
■ Storage: Airtight container.
■ Freeze: Uncooked doughnuts suitable.
■ Microwave: Not suitable.

Black Bottom Pie

From Kentucky, USA, the name of this pie comes simply from the fact that the base layer of filling is chocolate and the top half flavoured with rum.

90g butter
¼ cup caster sugar
1 egg
1 cup plain flour
¼ cup self-raising flour
½ cup thickened cream
30g dark chocolate, grated

FILLING

1 tablespoon gelatine
¼ cup milk
¼ cup caster sugar
3 teaspoons cornflour
1 cup milk, extra
3 eggs, separated
60g dark chocolate, melted
1 teaspoon vanilla essence
¼ cup caster sugar, extra

Cream butter and sugar in small bowl with electric mixer until just combined, add egg, beat until just combined, stir in sifted flours in 2 batches. Turn dough onto floured surface, knead gently until smooth; cover, refrigerate 30 minutes.

Roll pastry on floured surface large enough to fit 23cm pie plate. Place pastry in plate, trim edge, prick pastry all over with fork. Bake in moderately hot oven about 15 minutes or until browned; cool.

Spread chocolate custard into pastry case; refrigerate until firm. Spread vanilla custard into pastry case; refrigerate until firm. Spread whipped cream over custard, sprinkle with extra chocolate.

Filling: Sprinkle gelatine over milk in cup. Blend sugar and cornflour with extra milk in pan, stir over heat until mixture boils and thickens; remove from heat. Quickly stir in egg yolks, then gelatine mixture; stir until smooth.

Divide custard into 2 bowls. Stir chocolate into 1 bowl. Cover both bowls, cool to room temperature.

Stir essence into plain custard. Beat egg whites in small bowl with electric mixer until soft peaks form, gradually add extra sugar; beat until dissolved between additions. Fold egg white mixture into vanilla custard in 2 batches. Spread mixture over chocolate custard; refrigerate until firm.

Serves 6 to 8.

■ Recipe can be made a day ahead.
■ Storage: Covered, in refrigerator.
■ Freeze: Not suitable.
■ Microwave: Chocolate suitable.

Black Forest Cheesecake

The traditional Black Forest cake combination of cherries and rich chocolate came from the Swabia Black Forest region in Germany. We have adapted the recipe to make this very popular cheesecake.

250g plain uniced chocolate biscuits, finely crushed
125g butter, melted
3 teaspoons gelatine
½ cup water
250g packet cream cheese, softened
¾ cup caster sugar
1 tablespoon lemon juice
300ml carton thickened cream
425g can pitted black cherries

TOPPING

1 tablespoon cornflour
1 tablespoon caster sugar
1 tablespoon dark rum

Combine crumbs and butter in bowl, mix well; press over base and side of 20cm springform tin; refrigerate 30 minutes.

Sprinkle gelatine over water in cup, stand in small pan of simmering water, stir until dissolved; cool. Beat cream cheese, sugar and juice in small bowl with electric mixer until smooth and creamy; transfer to large bowl. Whip cream until soft peaks form, fold into cheese mixture; fold in gelatine mixture. Drain cherries, reserve ¾ cup syrup for topping.

Spoon one-third cheese mixture into crumb crust, top with half the cherries, then continue layering, ending with cheese mixture. Refrigerate several hours or until firm.

Spread topping over cheesecake, swirl gently into cheese mixture. Refrigerate until set. Decorate with extra whipped cream and extra cherries, if desired.

Topping: Blend cornflour and sugar with reserved syrup in pan. Stir over heat until mixture boils and thickens, stir in rum; cool 10 minutes before using.

Serves 6 to 8.

■ Recipe can be made 2 days ahead.
■ Storage: Covered, in refrigerator.
■ Freeze: Not suitable.
■ Microwave: Not suitable.

LEFT: From left: Black Forest Cheesecake, Black Bottom Pie.

Boiled Fruit Cake

Boiled fruit cake rapidly became a favourite Australian fruit cake as it is quicker to make and less expensive than the traditional baked versions.

The boiled fruit mixture is best left to cool slowly overnight.

2⅔ cups (500g) mixed dried fruit, chopped
½ cup water
1 cup brown sugar, firmly packed
125g butter
1 teaspoon mixed spice
½ teaspoon bicarbonate of soda
½ cup sweet sherry
1 egg, lightly beaten
1 cup plain flour
1 cup self-raising flour
blanched almonds
2 tablespoons sweet sherry, extra

Combine fruit, water, sugar, butter, spice and soda in large pan, stir over heat, without boiling, until sugar is dissolved and butter melted. Bring to boil, cover, simmer 5 minutes. Remove from heat, stir in sherry, cover, cool.

Grease deep 20cm round cake pan, line base and side with 2 thicknesses of paper, bringing paper 5cm above edge of pan. Stir egg and sifted flours into fruit mixture. Spread mixture into prepared pan, decorate top with almonds. Bake in moderately slow oven about 2 hours. Brush top of hot cake with extra sherry. Cover cake with foil, cool in pan.

■ Recipe can be made 2 weeks ahead.
■ Storage: Airtight container.
■ Freeze: Suitable.
■ Microwave: Boiled fruit mixture suitable.

Boiled Pineapple Fruit Cake

The traditional fruit cake took a unique turn in Australia where moist pineapple was used in addition to dried fruit. This sort of adaption was typical of pioneer cooking – plentiful local ingredients were often creatively incorporated into standard British recipes.

Keep, covered, in refrigerator if weather is wet or humid.

450g can crushed pineapple in heavy syrup
125g butter
1 cup caster sugar
2 cups (320g) sultanas
1 cup (160g) pitted chopped dates
½ cup glace cherries, halved
1 teaspoon bicarbonate of soda
2 eggs, lightly beaten
1 cup plain flour
1 cup self-raising flour
1 teaspoon mixed spice

Grease deep 20cm round cake pan, line base and side with 3 layers of paper, bringing paper 5cm above edge of pan.

Combine undrained pineapple, butter, sugar and fruit in pan, stir over heat, without boiling, until sugar is dissolved. Simmer, uncovered, about 10 minutes or until mixture is thick and syrupy. Remove from heat, stir in bicarbonate of soda, cool to room temperature.

Stir eggs, sifted flours and spice into fruit mixture, pour into prepared pan. Bake in moderately slow oven about 2¼ hours. Cover cake with foil, cool in pan.
■ Recipe can be made a week ahead.
■ Storage: Airtight container.
■ Freeze: Suitable.
■ Microwave: Boiled fruit mixture suitable.

LEFT: From back: Boiled Pineapple Fruit Cake, Boiled Fruit Cake.
ABOVE RIGHT: Bombe Alaska.

Above right: China from Mikasa.

Bombe Alaska

While moulded ice-creams have long been known as bombes because of their shape, Bombe Alaska was apparently invented by an American physicist around 1800, and was considered as a wonder of science more than a star of the culinary scene.

Use good quality ice-cream for this recipe. Be careful not to soften it too much, just enough to stir the fruit through quickly. It is important to keep freezing the dessert between the various stages or the ice-cream will melt.

17cm round sponge cake
1 tablespoon brandy
2 tablespoons jam
½ cup chopped red glace cherries
1½ litres (6 cups) softened vanilla ice-cream
½ cup chopped glace pineapple
½ cup chopped glace apricots
4 egg whites
1 cup caster sugar

Cover wooden board about 25cm square with foil. Place cake in centre, brush evenly with brandy, spread evenly with jam; freeze for 15 minutes.

Line aluminium pudding steamer (5 cup capacity) with foil, allowing 3cm to overhang edge. Rinse cherries under cold water, pat dry on absorbent paper.

Combine ice-cream and fruit in bowl, mix well. Spoon ice-cream mixture into prepared steamer, cover, freeze several hours or overnight until firm.

Turn ice-cream from steamer onto top of cake, peel away foil; return to freezer while making meringue.

Beat egg whites in small bowl with electric mixer until soft peaks form, gradually add sugar, beat until dissolved between additions. Spread meringue quickly all over ice-cream and cake. Return to freezer for 1 hour.

Bake in very hot oven about 3 minutes or until meringue is lightly browned. Serves 6 to 8.
■ Recipe can be made up to 12 hours ahead.
■ Storage: Freezer.
■ Microwave: Not suitable.

Boston Brown Bread

A moist, brown, American bread, this is cooked by steaming in round tins. In Puritan days, bakers often baked the pots of beans in their ovens for householders, and they added a bonus – a piece of brown bread. If you don't have the nut roll tins we suggest, you can use empty fruit cans for baking; cover with foil securely tied in place.

1 cup wholemeal plain flour
1 cup rye flour
1 teaspoon bicarbonate of soda
1¼ cups cornmeal
1 tablespoon sugar
¾ cup chopped raisins
1½ cups milk
½ cup treacle
1 teaspoon brown vinegar

Grease 2 x 8cm x 17cm nut roll tins. Sift flours and soda into large bowl, stir in cornmeal, sugar and raisins. Stir in combined milk, treacle and vinegar. Spoon mixture evenly into prepared tins, replace lids. Bake, standing upright, in moderate oven about 1 hour. Stand rolls 10 minutes before removing lids and turning onto wire rack to cool.

■ Recipe can be made 2 days ahead.
■ Storage: Airtight container.
■ Freeze: Suitable.
■ Microwave: Not suitable.

BELOW: Boston Bread
RIGHT: Brandy Snaps.

Right: China from Wedgwood; tray from Oneida Silverware; crystal from Bohemia Crystal.

Brandy Snaps

Some early recipes contained brandy and this, combined with the brittle texture, may have given these dainty biscuits their name.

Make 1 or 2 snaps first to establish a precise cooking time, then proceed with remaining mixture, cooking about 4 snaps on a tray at a time. Once you become confident, several trays can be baked at staggered times.

60g butter
⅓ cup brown sugar
2 tablespoons golden syrup
½ teaspoon ground ginger
½ cup plain flour
½ teaspoon lemon juice

Combine butter, sugar, golden syrup and ginger in pan, stir over low heat, without boiling, until butter is melted. Remove from heat, stir in sifted flour and juice. Drop level teaspoons of mixture about 6cm apart onto greased oven trays. Bake in moderate oven about 7 minutes or until snaps are bubbling and golden brown; remove from oven.

Slide a spatula under each snap, then wrap quickly around the handle of a wooden spoon. Remove spoon handle, then place snaps on wire rack to cool and become firm. Fill with whipped cream just before serving.
Makes about 20.

■ Recipe best made on day of serving.
■ Storage: Unfilled brandy snaps in airtight container.
■ Freeze: Not suitable.
■ Microwave: Not suitable.

Bread and Butter Pudding

Serve hot or cold with stewed or canned fruit and cream. Substitute any dried fruit of your choice in this recipe.

6 thin slices white bread
40g butter
3 eggs
¼ cup caster sugar
2½ cups milk
1 teaspoon vanilla essence
½ cup sultanas
ground nutmeg or ground cinnamon

Trim crusts from bread, butter each slice, cut into 4 triangles. Arrange a layer of triangles, butter side up, overlapping slightly, along centre of shallow, ovenproof dish (8 cup capacity). Place another row triangles between first layer, in opposite direction to the first layer.

Whisk eggs, sugar, milk and essence together in bowl, pour half the custard mixture over bread, stand 10 minutes.

Whisk remaining egg mixture again, add sultanas; pour into dish. Sprinkle with nutmeg or cinnamon. Stand dish in baking dish, with enough boiling water to come halfway up side of dish. Bake, uncovered, in moderately slow oven about 50 minutes or until custard is set. Serves 4 to 6.

■ Recipe can be made a day ahead.
■ Storage: Covered, in refrigerator.
■ Freeze: Not suitable.
■ Microwave: Not suitable.

Bread Pudding

Here is an easy, inexpensive way to use 2 or 3 day old bread. We've used white bread, but a light wholemeal bread is also good. Fruit can be varied to suit your own taste; allow 2 cups (320g) chopped mixed dried fruit instead, if desired.

1½ loaves (about 900g) stale sliced white bread
4 cups water
1 cup (160g) sultanas
½ cup chopped raisins
¼ cup currants
¼ cup chopped glace cherries
2 tablespoons mixed peel
1 cup caster sugar
125g butter, melted
1 tablespoon mixed spice
1 egg, lightly beaten

Remove and discard crusts from bread. Chop bread, place into large bowl, add water, cover, stand 30 minutes.

Place bread in larger strainer, press out as much liquid as possible; discard liquid.

Combine bread, fruit, sugar, butter, spice and egg in bowl, mix with wooden spoon until combined. Spread into greased deep (6 cup capacity) ovenproof dish. Bake, uncovered, in moderate oven about 1½ hours or until firm. Serves 8.

■ Recipe can be made a day ahead.
■ Storage: Covered, in refrigerator.
■ Freeze: Not suitable.
■ Microwave: Not suitable.

Butterscotch Curls

A rich butterscotch mixture of brown sugar, butter and nuts makes a simple scone dough special. Curls are best eaten hot, split and served with more butter.

60g butter
⅓ cup brown sugar
¼ cup chopped walnuts
3 cups self-raising flour
90g butter, extra
1¼ cups milk, approximately
⅓ cup brown sugar, extra

BELOW LEFT: From left: Bread and Butter Pudding, Bread Pudding.
LEFT: Butterscotch Buttons.
BELOW: Butterscotch Curls.

Below left: Table and butter press from Woollahra Antiques Centre; cloth from Country Road Homewares.
Below: China from Wedgwood; silver from Oneida Silverware; cloth from Redelman & Son.

Grease deep 20cm round cake pan. Beat butter and sugar together in small bowl with wooden spoon until just combined, spread over base of prepared pan; sprinkle with nuts.

Sift flour into bowl, rub in half the extra butter. Add enough milk to mix to a firm dough. Knead gently on lightly floured surface until smooth. Roll dough to 23cm x 28cm rectangle. Melt remaining extra butter, brush over dough, sprinkle with extra sugar. Roll up as for Swiss roll, from long side. Cut into 10 rounds, place cut side up in prepared pan. Bake in moderately hot oven about 25 minutes.
Makes 10.

■ Recipe can be prepared 3 hours ahead.
■ Storage: Covered at room temperature.
■ Freeze: Uncooked curls suitable.
■ Microwave: Not suitable.

Butterscotch Buttons

125g butter
1 teaspoon vanilla essence
½ cup brown sugar, firmly packed
1 tablespoon golden syrup
1¼ cups self-raising flour

Beat butter, essence, sugar and golden syrup in small bowl with electric mixer until light and fluffy; stir in sifted flour. Roll 2 level teaspoons of mixture into a ball, place about 5cm apart on greased oven trays, flatten slightly with fork. Repeat with remaining mixture. Bake in slow oven about 30 minutes or until firm, lift onto wire rack to cool.
Makes about 40.

■ Recipe can be made a week ahead.
■ Storage: Airtight container.
■ Freeze: Suitable.
■ Microwave: Not suitable.

Caramel Banana Tart

The tropic-loving banana, of which there are hundreds of varieties, used to be called the 'apple of paradise' – apparently the Garden of Eden's infamous serpent is said to have hidden in a bunch. It is certainly hard to resist the temptation of this luscious, cream and coconut smothered tart.

1 cup plain flour
60g butter
2 tablespoons caster sugar
1 egg yolk
1 tablespoon water, approximately
2 bananas, thinly sliced
300ml carton thickened cream, whipped
1 tablespoon coconut

FILLING
1 cup brown sugar, firmly packed
125g butter
1 tablespoon boiling water
¼ cup cornflour
1 cup milk
2 egg yolks
1 teaspoon vanilla essence

Lightly grease 24cm loose-based flan tin. Sift flour into bowl, rub in butter; mix in sugar and yolk with fingertips, then enough water to bind ingredients together. Knead dough gently on floured surface until smooth, cover, refrigerate for 30 minutes.

Roll dough on lightly floured surface large enough to line prepared tin; trim edges. Line pastry with paper, fill with dried beans or rice. Bake in moderately hot oven 10 minutes, remove paper and beans, bake further 7 minutes or until pastry is lightly browned; cool.

Pour filling into pastry case; top with bananas, spread with cream, sprinkle with coconut; refrigerate before serving.
Filling: Combine sugar, butter and water in pan, stir over heat, without boiling, until butter is melted and sugar dissolved. Stir in blended cornflour and milk, stir over heat until mixture boils and thickens. Remove from heat, stir in yolks and essence; cover, cool.
Serves 6 to 8.
▉ Recipe can be made a day ahead.
▉ Storage: Covered, in refrigerator.
▉ Freeze: Not suitable.
▉ Microwave: Not suitable.

Caramel Bananas

100g butter
⅓ cup brown sugar
¾ cup caster sugar
2 tablespoons water
½ cup thickened cream
4 ripe bananas, sliced

Heat butter in pan, add sugars and water, stir over heat, without boiling, until sugar is dissolved, stir in cream, bring to boil, add bananas. Serve with cream or ice-cream, if desired.
Serves 4.
▉ Recipe best made just before serving.
▉ Freeze: Not suitable.
▉ Microwave: Not suitable.

LEFT: From top: Caramel Banana Tart, Caramel Bananas.

China from Royal Doulton.

Caramel Chocolate Slice

The caramel filling must be stirred constantly during cooking for perfect results.

1 cup self-raising flour
1 cup (90g) coconut
1 cup brown sugar, firmly packed
125g butter, melted

FILLING
400g can sweetened condensed milk
30g butter
2 tablespoons golden syrup

TOPPING
125g dark chocolate, chopped
30g butter

Lightly grease 20cm x 30cm lamington pan. Combine sifted flour, coconut and sugar in bowl, add butter, stir until combined. Press mixture over base of prepared pan. Bake in moderate oven 15 minutes. Pour hot filling over hot base, return to oven 10 minutes; cool.

Spread warm topping over filling, stand at room temperature until set.

Filling: Combine milk, butter and golden syrup in pan, stir over low heat, without boiling, about 15 minutes or until mixture is golden brown.

Topping: Combine chocolate and butter in pan, stir over low heat until smooth.

■ Recipe can be made 3 days ahead.
■ Storage: Airtight container.
■ Freeze: Not suitable.
■ Microwave: Topping suitable.

LEFT: From top: Caramel Corn Flake Chews, Caramel Chocolate Slice.

ABOVE RIGHT: Carrot Cake.

Left: China from Royal Doulton; cutlery from Oneida Silverware.

Caramel Corn Flake Chews

These biscuits do not contain any flour.

125g butter
½ cup brown sugar, firmly packed
½ cup caster sugar
½ cup coconut
3 cups Corn Flakes, lightly crushed
1 egg, lightly beaten
½ cup finely chopped mixed nuts

Melt butter in large pan, add sugars, cook, stirring, until combined. Remove from heat, stir in coconut, Corn Flakes, egg and nuts, stir gently until combined. Place level tablespoons of mixture about 3cm apart on lightly greased oven trays. Bake in moderate oven about 15 minutes or until golden brown. Stand 5 minutes before removing from trays to cool on wire rack.
Makes about 25.

■ Recipe can be made a week ahead.
■ Storage: Airtight container.
■ Freeze: Suitable.
■ Microwave: Not suitable.

Carrot Cake

Believed to be of American origin, carrot cakes started to become really popular in the 1950s, and became trendy in Australia about the early 1980s. The cream cheese frosting adds richness.

Use 3 medium carrots for this recipe.

1 cup oil
1⅓ cups brown sugar, firmly packed
3 eggs
3 cups coarsely grated carrot
1 cup (120g) chopped walnuts or pecans
½ cup chopped raisins
2½ cups self-raising flour
½ teaspoon bicarbonate of soda
2 teaspoons mixed spice

CREAM CHEESE FROSTING
30g butter
80g packaged cream cheese, softened
1 teaspoon grated lemon rind
1 tablespoon lemon juice
1½ cups icing sugar

Grease 15cm x 25cm loaf pan, line base with paper; grease paper. Beat oil, sugar and eggs in small bowl with electric mixer until thick and creamy. Transfer mixture to large bowl, stir in carrot, nuts and raisins, then sifted dry ingredients.

Pour mixture into prepared pan, bake in moderate oven 45 minutes. Cover loosely with foil, bake about further 45 minutes. Stand a few minutes before turning onto wire rack to cool. Top cold cake with cream cheese frosting.

Cream Cheese Frosting: Beat butter, cheese, rind and juice in small bowl with electric mixer, beat until light and fluffy; gradually beat in sifted icing sugar.

■ Recipe can be made 2 days ahead.
■ Storage: Airtight container.
■ Freeze: Suitable
■ Microwave: Not suitable.

Cheesecake

Since the earliest times, cheesecake has been a popular treat, and there is an amazing variety of ways to make it. A tremendous favourite in the United States, cheesecake caught on in a big way in Australia in the 1960s. Ours is an easy recipe with a lingering, light lemon taste and velvety texture.

250g plain sweet biscuits
125g butter, melted
FILLING
3 x 250g packet cream cheese, softened
½ cup caster sugar
3 eggs
3 teaspoons grated lemon rind
¼ cup lemon juice

Grease 20cm springform tin. Blend, process or crush biscuits finely, stir in butter. Using a flat-bottomed glass, press crumb mixture evenly over base and side of prepared tin, refrigerate 30 minutes or until firm.

Place springform tin on oven tray, pour filling into tin. Bake in moderately slow oven about 50 minutes, or until firm. Cool in oven with door ajar.

Cover cheesecake, refrigerate several hours or overnight before serving. Serve with whipped cream, sprinkle with ground nutmeg, if desired.

Filling: Beat cheese and sugar in medium bowl with electric mixer until smooth. Add eggs 1 at a time, beat well between additions. Add rind and juice, beat until mixture is creamy.

■ Recipe can be made 3 days ahead.
■ Storage: Covered, in refrigerator.
■ Freeze: Suitable.
■ Microwave: Not suitable.

BELOW: From left: Cheesecake, Cheesecakes.
RIGHT: Chelsea Buns.

Below: China from Royal Doulton. Right: Silverware from Oneida Silverware.

Cheesecakes

Small, delicate cheesecakes seem to have originated in England, and were made using rich, creamy, fresh cows' milk. To a pint of milk warm from the cow or slightly heated, a teaspoonful of rennet was added; the curds left were strained off in muslin. To this was added ingredients for the cake layer. Cheesecakes had nothing to do with cheese except that curds are akin to cheese. In some places these cakes were called Maids of Honour; one story says that Anne Boleyn produced them to please her husband King Henry VIII.

1 cup plain flour
60g butter
¼ cup caster sugar
1 egg yolk
1 teaspoon water, approximately
2 tablespoons jam, approximately

CAKE MIXTURE

60g butter
1 teaspoon vanilla essence
⅓ cup caster sugar
1 egg
¾ cup self-raising flour
¼ cup milk

Lightly grease 2 x 12 hole shallow patty pans. Sift flour into bowl, rub in butter, stir in sugar. Mix in egg yolk and enough water to make ingredients cling together. Press dough into ball, knead gently on lightly floured surface, cover, refrigerate 30 minutes.

Roll dough on lightly floured surface, until 2mm thick. Cut into 6cm rounds; place into prepared pans.

Place about ¼ teaspoon jam into each pastry case, top with 3 level teaspoons of cake mixture.

Roll pastry scraps, cut into thin strips, twist pastry strips, place on top of cake mixture. Bake in moderate oven about 15 minutes or until lightly browned.

Cake Mixture: Cream butter, essence and sugar in small bowl with electric mixer, until lightly and fluffy; add egg, beat until combined. Stir in sifted flour and milk.

Makes 24.

- Recipe can be made a day ahead.
- Storage: Airtight container.
- Freeze: Suitable.
- Microwave: Not suitable.

Chelsea Buns

Long ago, when the London suburb of Chelsea was a village in the country, buns were made and sold at the Chelsea Bun House (it was demolished in 1838). Fashionable people, even royalty, would gather there to enjoy the delicious fare.

2 x 7g sachets granulated yeast
1 teaspoon caster sugar
1 teaspoon plain flour
1½ cups warm milk
2 cups (280g) currants
1 teaspoon grated lemon rind
1 teaspoon ground cinnamon
1 egg, lightly beaten
4 cups plain flour, extra
125g butter, melted
⅔ cup brown sugar, firmly packed
1 tablespoon caster sugar, extra

ICING

1 cup icing sugar
1 tablespoon milk, approximately
pink food colouring

Grease deep 23cm square cake pan. Combine yeast, caster sugar, flour and milk in bowl; cover, stand in warm place about 10 minutes or until mixture is frothy.

Place currants in pan, cover with water, bring to boil, remove from heat, cover, cool.

Drain currants well, combine in small bowl with rind and cinnamon. Whisk egg into yeast mixture. Sift extra flour into large bowl, stir in yeast mixture, cover, stand in warm place about 40 minutes or until dough is doubled in size.

Turn dough onto lightly floured surface, knead about 3 minutes or until smooth. Roll dough to 30cm x 40cm rectangle. Brush with quarter of the butter, sprinkle evenly with one-third of the brown sugar.

Fold 1 end of the dough to come two-thirds of the way up the dough, fold over top third to cover first fold. Turn

dough halfway around to have open ends facing you.

Roll dough to 30cm x 40cm rectangle. Repeat folding as before, using same amount of butter and brown sug-

ar. Turn dough half-way round, roll to 30cm x 40cm rectangle. Brush dough with half the remaining butter, sprinkle with remaining brown sugar and currant mixture.

Roll dough firmly from long side like a Swiss roll. Cut dough evenly into 9 pieces. Place buns, cut side up, into prepared pan, sprinkle with extra caster sugar. Stand, uncovered, in warm place

about 20 minutes or until buns have risen slightly.

Drizzle buns with remaining butter, bake in moderately hot oven 5 minutes, reduce heat to moderate, bake further 25 minutes or until buns are golden brown. Turn buns onto wire rack, drizzle a little icing onto each bun; cool.

Icing: Sift icing sugar into bowl, stir in enough milk to form a thin, smooth paste, tint with pink colouring.

Makes 9.

- Recipe can be made 4 hours ahead.
- Storage: Airtight container.
- Freeze: Suitable.
- Microwave: Not suitable.

Cherries Jubilee

Easy and elegant, Cherries Jubilee is thought to have royal connections. Apparently Queen Victoria was so fond of cherries that she had an orchard of them planted at Windsor, and this dessert may have been created for her Jubilee celebrations.

425g can pitted black cherries
1 tablespoon caster sugar
1 cinnamon stick
2 teaspoons arrowroot
1 tablespoon water
⅓ cup brandy

Drain cherries, reserve syrup. Combine syrup, sugar and cinnamon in pan, cook, stirring, until mixture boils; simmer, uncovered without stirring, 2 minutes; strain, discard cinnamon.

Return syrup to pan, stir in blended arrowroot and water, cook, stirring until mixture boils and thickens slightly. Add cherries, stir until heated through.

Heat brandy, add to sauce, set aflame. Serve immediately with ice-cream.
Serves 4.

VARIATION

Fresh cherries may be substituted for canned cherries in this recipe. Remove stones from 500g cherries, place in pan, add 1 cup water and ¼ cup sugar, simmer until cherries are just soft. Use this syrup in place of the syrup for the can.
■ Recipe best made just before serving.
■ Storage: Covered, in refrigerator.
■ Freeze: Not suitable.
■ Microwave: Cherry mixture suitable.

LEFT: Cherries Jubilee.
RIGHT: Cherry Cake.

Left: Silverware from Oneida Silverware; fabric from Redelman & Son.

Cherry Cake

The subtle richness of almonds is brilliant with nice-to-bite cherry chunks.

180g butter, softened
1 teaspoon almond essence
¾ cup caster sugar
3 eggs
2 cups self-raising flour
2 tablespoons packaged ground almonds
⅓ cup milk
½ cup sour cream
1 cup (210g) red glace cherries, quartered

Grease deep 20cm round cake pan, line base with paper, grease paper. Beat butter, essence and sugar in small bowl with electric mixer until light and fluffy, beat in eggs 1 at a time, beating well between additions. Stir in sifted flour and almonds in 2 batches with milk and sour cream; stir in cherries.

Spread mixture into prepared pan. Bake in moderate oven about 1¼ hours. Stand cake few minutes before turning onto wire rack to cool. Sprinkle with sifted icing sugar, if desired.

■ Recipe can be made a day ahead.
■ Storage: Airtight container.
■ Freeze: Suitable.
■ Microwave: Not suitable.

Chester Squares

Believed to be of English origin, the surprise ingredient here is crumbled fruit cake. It's a delicious way of using up stale fruit cake, or creating some variety with that beautiful Christmas cake.

90g butter
¼ cup caster sugar
1 egg
2 tablespoons self-raising flour
1¼ cups plain flour
2 teaspoons caster sugar, extra

FILLING
90g butter
⅓ cup caster sugar
1 egg
2 tablespoons apricot jam
2 cups (about 250g) moist fruit cake crumbs
½ cup self-raising flour
2 teaspoons mixed spice
½ cup milk

Grease 20cm x 30cm lamington pan. Beat butter and sugar in small bowl with electric mixer until just combined, add egg, beat until combined. Fold in sifted flours in 2 batches. Turn dough onto floured surface, knead until smooth. Divide dough in half, cover, refrigerate 30 minutes.

Roll half the pastry between sheets of greaseproof paper large enough to fit base of prepared pan, trim edges. Spread filling evenly over pastry base. Roll remaining pastry large enough to cover filling, place over filling, trim edges. Brush pastry with water, sprinkle with extra sugar, prick with fork. Bake in moderate oven about 45 minutes or until golden brown. Stand slice 10 minutes before turning onto wire rack to cool.

Filling: Beat butter, sugar and egg in small bowl with electric mixer until light and fluffy, stir in jam and crumbs, then sifted flour, spice and milk.

■ Recipe can be made 4 days ahead.
■ Storage: Airtight container.
■ Freeze: Suitable.
■ Microwave: Not suitable.

RIGHT: Chester Squares.
ABOVE RIGHT: Chocolate Brownies.
ABOVE FAR RIGHT: Chocolate Blancmange.

Right: China from Royal Doulton; tablecloth from Belinda's Corner.

Chocolate Brownies

An American creation, brownies are extravagantly rich and luscious, and usually made with lashings of chocolate.

30g butter
250g dark chocolate, finely chopped
80g butter, extra
2 teaspoons vanilla essence
1 cup brown sugar, firmly packed
2 eggs
½ cup plain flour
½ cup chopped roasted hazelnuts
⅓ cup sour cream

CHOCOLATE ICING
125g dark chocolate, chopped
60g unsalted butter

Grease deep 19cm square cake pan, line base with paper; grease paper.

Melt butter in pan, add chocolate, stir over low heat until chocolate is melted; cool 5 minutes.

Beat extra butter, essence and sugar in small bowl with electric mixer until light and fluffy, beat in eggs 1 at a time. Transfer mixture to large bowl.

Stir in sifted flour, then chocolate mixture, nuts and cream. Spread mixture into prepared pan, bake in moderate oven about 45 minutes; cool in pan.

Turn slice from pan, remove paper. Spread slice with chocolate icing; cut when set.

Chocolate Icing: Melt chocolate and butter over simmering water, cool to room temperature. Beat with wooden spoon until thick and spreadable.

■ Recipe can be made 3 days ahead.
■ Storage: Airtight container.
■ Freeze: Suitable.
■ Microwave: Butter and chocolate mixtures suitable.

Chocolate Blancmange

Of early French origin, blancmange was made with almond milk and gelatine, literally 'white food'. However, today we use ordinary milk and cornflour, and add flavourings to our taste.

60g dark chocolate, chopped
⅓ cup cornflour
2½ cups milk
2 tablespoons caster sugar
1 teaspoon vanilla essence

Place chocolate in heatproof bowl, place oven pan of simmering water, stir chocolate until melted; cool 5 minutes.

Blend cornflour with ½ cup of the milk in bowl. Add remaining milk to pan wtih sugar, stir until nearly boiling. Remove from heat, stir cornflour mixture into milk mixture; cook, stirring, until mixture boils and thickens. Remove from heat, stir in chocolate and essence; stir until smooth. Pour into 4 glasses (1 cup capacity), cover, cool. Refrigerate blancmange several hours or overnight. Serve with cream and chocolate curls, if desired.
Serves 4.
■ Recipe best made a day ahead.
■ Storage: Covered, in refrigerator.
■ Freeze: Not suitable.
■ Microwave: Suitable.

Chocolate Chip Cookies

One story suggests that these were created by a housewife in Massachusetts, USA, in 1929. They are also known as Toll House Cookies.

90g butter
1 teaspoon vanilla essence
⅓ cup caster sugar
⅓ cup brown sugar
1 egg
½ cup self-raising flour
¾ cup plain flour
¾ cup Choc Bits
½ cup chopped pecans or walnuts
1 tablespoon milk

BELOW: From left: Chocolate Chip Cookies, Chocolate Crackles.
RIGHT: From left: Cream Puffs, Chocolate Eclairs.

Below: Blue and white plates and jug from Accoutrement.
Right: China from Woodheath Pty Ltd; tablecloth from Belinda's Corner; table from Woollahra Antiques Centre.

Beat butter, essence and sugars in a small bowl with electric mixer until light and fluffy, beat in egg. Stir in flours, Choc Bits, nuts and milk. Drop level tablespoons of mixture onto lightly greased oven trays, about 3cm apart. Bake in moderate oven about 12 minutes or until firm and lightly browned. Stand on trays 5 minutes before lifting onto wire racks to cool.
Makes about 30.
■ Recipe can be made 4 days ahead.
■ Storage: Airtight container.
■ Freeze: Suitable.
■ Microwave: Not suitable.

Chocolate Crackles

An Australian favourite, this quick treat is great for children's parties.

4 cups (140g) Rice Bubbles
1 cup (90g) coconut
⅔ cup cocoa
1½ cups icing sugar
250g Copha

Combine Rice Bubbles, coconut, sifted cocoa and icing sugar in large bowl. Melt Copha in pan over low heat, pour over dry ingredients; mix well. Spoon 2 level tablespoons of mixture into paper patty cases; refrigerate until set.
Makes about 25.
■ Recipe can be made 2 days ahead.
■ Storage: Covered, in refrigerator.
■ Freeze: Not suitable.
■ Microwave: Not suitable.

Chocolate Eclairs

Eclair, meaning lightning or flash of light, is the traditional name for a French choux pastry-cake. Cream puffs are also made from choux pastry.

Both can be filled with cream flavoured to suit your taste.

80g butter, chopped
1 cup water
1 cup plain flour
4 eggs, lightly beaten
125g dark chocolate, melted
60g unsalted butter, melted

CHANTILLY CREAM
300ml carton thickened cream, whipped
1 teaspoon vanilla essence
2 tablespoons icing sugar, sifted

Combine butter and water in pan, bring to boil. Add sifted flour all at once, stir vigorously over heat until mixture leaves side of pan and forms a smooth ball.

Transfer mixture to small bowl of electric mixer, beat in eggs 1 at a time, beating well between additions. Mixture should be glossy.

Using piping bag fitted with 1½cm plain tube, pipe 11cm lengths of pastry about 3cm apart onto lightly greased oven trays. Bake in hot oven 10 minutes, reduce to moderate, bake a further 10 minutes or until pastry is lightly browned and crisp. Cut eclairs in half, remove any soft centre. Return to moderate oven for a few minutes to dry out; cool on wire rack.

Dip top half of each eclair in combined chocolate and butter, then join halves with chantilly cream just before serving.

Chantilly Cream: Combine all ingredients in small bowl, cover, refrigerate 30 minutes. Beat cream mixture with electric mixer or rotary beater until thick.

Makes about 15.

VARIATION

Cream Puffs: Make pastry as indicated above. Drop 2 tablespoons of mixture about 5cm apart onto lightly greased oven trays. Proceed as for eclairs.

Split cold puffs in half, join with chantilly cream just before serving. Dust lightly with a little extra sifted icing sugar.

■ Pastry can be cooked a day ahead.
■ Storage: Unfilled eclairs or puffs in airtight container.
■ Freeze: Unfilled eclairs or puffs suitable.
■ Microwave: Not suitable.

Chocolate Mousse

The essence of a mousse is lightness, indicated by its French name meaning foam or froth. This favourite is delicate yet rich with cream and chocolate.

200g dark chocolate, chopped
30g unsalted butter
3 eggs, separated
300ml carton thickened cream,
   whipped

Place chocolate in heatproof bowl, place over pan of simmering water, stir chocolate until melted, remove from heat. Add butter, stir until melted, stir in egg yolks, 1 at a time; transfer mixture to large bowl, cover, cool.

Beat egg whites in small bowl with electric mixer until soft peaks form. Fold the cream and egg whites into chocolate mixture in 2 batches. Pour mixture into 6 serving dishes (⅔ cup capacity), refrigerate several hours or overnight.

Serve with extra whipped cream and chocolate curls, if desired. Serves 6.

■ Recipe best made a day ahead.
■ Storage: Covered, in refrigerator.
■ Freeze: Not suitable.
■ Microwave: Chocolate and butter suitable.

Chocolate Peppermint Slice

1½ **cups self-raising flour**
½ **cup coconut**
½ **cup brown sugar, firmly packed**
125g **butter, melted**

FILLING
30g **Copha**
1¾ **cups icing sugar**
2 **tablespoons milk**
½ **teaspoon peppermint essence**

TOPPING
125g **dark chocolate, chopped**
30g **butter**

Lightly grease 20cm x 30cm lamington pan, line with paper, grease paper. Combine sifted flour, coconut and sugar in bowl, add butter, stir until combined. Press mixture over base of prepared pan. Bake in moderate oven 20 minutes. Spread with filling while hot; cool. Spread with topping, refrigerate until set.
Filling: Melt Copha in pan, stir in sifted icing sugar, milk and essence.
Topping: Combine chocolate and butter in pan, stir over low heat until smooth.

■ Recipe can be made 3 days ahead.
■ Storage: Covered, in refrigerator.
■ Freeze: Not suitable.
■ Microwave: Topping suitable.

Chocolate Self-Saucing Pudding

In this recipe, the mixture separates during cooking to form a cake layer over the smooth, creamy sauce.
60g **butter**
½ **cup milk**
1 **teaspoon vanilla essence**
¾ **cup caster sugar**
1 **cup self-raising flour**
1 **tablespoon cocoa**
¾ **cup brown sugar, firmly packed**

1 **tablespoon cocoa, extra**
2 **cups boiling water**

Combine butter and milk in large pan, stir over heat until butter is melted. Remove from heat, stir in essence and caster sugar, then sifted flour and cocoa. Spread mixture into greased ovenproof dish (6 cup capacity). Sift brown sugar and extra cocoa over mixture, gently pour over boiling water. Bake in moderate oven about 40 minutes.
Serves 4 to 6.
■ Recipe best made just before serving.
■ Freeze. Not suitable.
■ Microwave: Suitable.

LEFT: From left: Chocolate Mousse, Chocolate Self-Saucing Pudding.
ABOVE: Chocolate Peppermint Slice.
Above: Tablecloth from The Cottage Manner.

Cinnamon Teacake

To make a light and fluffy teacake, it is important to cream the butter, essence, sugar and egg thoroughly until it is as light and white as possible. Teacakes are best eaten warm from the oven.

60g butter
1 teaspoon vanilla essence
⅔ cup caster sugar
1 egg
1 cup self-raising flour
⅓ cup milk
10g butter, melted, extra
1 teaspoon ground cinnamon
1 tablespoon caster sugar, extra

Grease deep 20cm round cake pan, line base with paper, grease paper. Beat butter, essence, sugar and egg in small bowl with electric mixer until light and fluffy. Stir in sifted flour and milk, stir gently until smooth. Spread mixture into prepared pan. Bake in moderate oven about 30 minutes. Turn onto wire rack, brush with extra butter and sprinkle with combined cinnamon and extra sugar while hot. Serve warm with butter.

■ Recipe best made on day of serving.
■ Storage: Airtight container.
■ Freeze: Suitable.
■ Microwave: Not suitable.

Coconut Cake

125g butter
1 teaspoon coconut essence
¾ cup caster sugar
2 egg whites
⅓ cup hot water
1 cup (90g) coconut
1¼ cups self-raising flour
1 tablespoon coconut, extra

ICING
1 cup icing sugar
1 teaspoon soft butter
1 tablespoon milk, approximately
pink food colouring

Grease 14cm x 21cm loaf pan, line base with paper, grease paper. Beat butter, essence and sugar in small bowl with electric mixer until light and fluffy, add egg whites, beat well. Stir in combined water and coconut, then sifted flour. Spread mixture into prepared pan, bake in moderate oven about 1 hour.

Stand few minutes before turning cake onto wire rack to cool. Spread cake with icing, sprinkle with extra coconut.

Icing: Sift icing sugar into small heatproof bowl, stir in butter and enough milk to form a stiff paste, tint with colouring. Stir over hot water until spreadable.

- Recipe can be made 3 days ahead.
- Storage: Airtight container.
- Freeze: Suitable.
- Microwave: Not suitable.

Coconut Ice

One of Australia's favourite sweets, this creamy favourite is quick and easy, and needs no cooking.

4¾ cups (760g) icing sugar
2½ cups (225g) coconut
400g can sweetened condensed milk
1 egg white, lightly beaten
pink food colouring

Line deep 19cm square cake pan with foil. Sift icing sugar into large bowl, stir in coconut then milk and egg white, stir until well combined. Press half mixture into prepared pan. Tint remaining mixture pink, press evenly over first layer; cover, refrigerate several hours before cutting.

- Recipe can be made a week ahead.
- Storage: Covered, in refrigerator.
- Freeze: Not suitable.

BELOW LEFT: Cinnamon Teacake.
BELOW: From left: Coconut Cake, Coconut Ice.

Below left: Flower jug and butter dish from The Cottage Manner; napkin and tablecloth from Country Road; cutlery from Wirths. Below: Cake tin and jug cover from the Cottage Manner.

College Pudding

Believed to be of English origin, this is a steamed pudding where jam is put into the steamer first then topped with the pudding mixture; use the jam of your choice.

¼ cup jam
125g butter
1 teaspoon vanilla essence
½ cup caster sugar
2 eggs
2 cups self-raising flour
½ cup milk

Grease aluminium pudding steamer (8 cup capacity). Spoon jam into base of steamer. Beat butter, essence and sugar in small bowl with electric mixer until light and fluffy, beat in eggs 1 at a time, beat until combined. Transfer mixture to large bowl, stir in sifted flour and milk in 2 batches. Spread mixture into steamer, cover with greased foil, secure with string or lid.

Place steamer in large pan with enough boiling water to come half-way up side of steamer; boil, covered about 1½ hours or until firm. Replenish water as necessary. Serve with custard, cream or ice-cream.
Serves 6 to 8.
■ Recipe best made just before serving.
■ Freeze: Not suitable.
■ Microwave: Not suitable.

LEFT: From top: Creamed Rice, College Pudding.
ABOVE: Cream Horns.

Above: China from Royal Doulton; tea strainer from Strachan.

Cream Horns

The crisp pastry shapes are quickly made by wrapping strips around cream horn tins. You can vary the jam you use and flavour the cream with liqueur or spirits to complement the chosen jam, if desired.

375g packet frozen puff pastry, thawed
milk
½ cup jam

CHANTILLY CREAM
1 tablespoon icing sugar
1 teaspoon vanilla essence
300ml carton thickened cream

Lightly grease 8 x 5cm x 15cm cream horn tins. Roll pastry thinly on lightly floured surface to a rectangle, cut into 2cm strips. Moisten 1 edge of each strip with water. Starting at point of cone, wind strips around cone, overlapping the moistened edge; do not stretch pastry. Join edge of strips with a little water. Bring pastry to about 1cm from end of cone. Repeat with remaining pastry.

Place cones about 3cm apart on lightly greased oven tray, brush pastry lightly and evenly with milk. Bake in moderate oven 30 minutes, slip tins from pastry horns, bake about further 5 minutes or until pastry is crisp. Cool on wire rack. Spoon jam into pastry horns, spoon or pipe chantilly cream into horns just before serving. Dust with a little icing sugar, if desired.

Chantilly Cream: combine all ingredients in bowl, refrigerate 30 minutes. Beat with electric mixer or rotary beater until soft peaks form.

Makes 8.

■ Pastry horns can be made a day ahead.
■ Storage: Unfilled pastry horns in airtight container.
■ Freeze: Unfilled pastry horns suitable.
■ Microwave: Not suitable.

Creamed Rice

It is important to use full-cream milk in this recipe; cook rice slowly for creamiest results. Serve with fruit of your choice.

1 litre (4 cups) milk
⅔ cup caster sugar
½ cup short-grain rice
1 teaspoon vanilla essence

Combine milk and sugar in medium pan, bring to boil, stirring. Gradually stir rice into boiling milk. Cover pan tightly, cook over low heat, stirring occasionally for about 1 hour or until rice is tender and most of the liquid is absorbed. Stir in essence. Serve warm or cold.

Serves 4 to 6.

■ Recipe can be made a day ahead.
■ Storage: Covered, in refrigerator.
■ Freeze: Not suitable.
■ Microwave: Suitable.

Crepes Suzette

Perhaps the most famous, fine 'pancakes' in the world, these have a fabulous, romantic history involving high society and wonderful dinners. For a spectacular finale, you can flame them restaurant-style at the table in a chafing dish, but always be careful when igniting the crepes.

¾ cup plain flour
3 eggs
2 tablespoons oil
¾ cup milk
SAUCE
125g butter
½ cup caster sugar
1½ cups fresh orange juice, strained
2 tablespoons lemon juice
⅓ cup Grand Marnier

Sift flour into medium bowl, make well in centre, add eggs and oil, gradually stir in milk, whisk until smooth; cover, stand 1 hour.

Heat heavy-based greased crepe pan. Pour 2 to 3 tablespoons of batter into pan from a jug, turn pan so batter coats base evenly. Cook slowly, loosening edge with spatula until crepe is lightly browned underneath. Turn crepe, brown other side, remove from pan; cover to keep warm. Repeat with remaining batter, fold crepes in half, then in half again.

Place crepes in sauce, heat through gently. Serve crepes with sauce. Serve with orange segments and whipped cream, if desired.

Sauce: Melt butter in pan, add sugar, cook, stirring, until sugar mixture begins to brown. Add juices, cook, stirring, until caramelised sugar is dissolved. Bring to boil, add liqueur, remove from heat, ignite.

Serves 4 to 6.
- Recipe best made just before serving.
- Freeze: Crepes suitable.
- Microwave: Not suitable.

LEFT: Crepes Suzette.
ABOVE RIGHT: Custard Tart.

Above right: Milk jug and cake server from David Jones.

Custard Tart

The secret to making a perfect custard tart is to make sure the pastry case is without cracks and joins and you will have a perfect tart every time.

1¼ cups plain flour
¼ cup self-raising flour
¼ cup caster sugar
90g butter
1 egg
2 teaspoons water, approximately
ground nutmeg
CUSTARD
3 eggs, lightly beaten
1 teaspoon vanilla essence
2 tablespoons caster sugar
2 cups milk

Sift flours and sugar into bowl, rub in butter. Add egg and enough water to make ingredients cling together. Press dough into ball, knead on floured surface until smooth, cover, refrigerate 30 minutes.

Roll dough on lightly floured surface large enough to line 23cm pie plate, trim edges. Lift pastry into pie plate, gently ease into side of plate, trim edges. Use scraps of pastry to make a double layer of pastry around edge of plate, join pastry strips with a little water. Trim edges, pinch a frill around edge of pastry.

Place pie plate on oven tray, line pastry with paper, fill with dried beans or rice. Bake in moderately hot oven 10 minutes, remove paper and beans, bake further 10 minutes or until pastry is lightly browned; cool pastry.

Pour custard into pastry case, bake in moderate oven 15 minutes. Sprinkle custard evenly with nutmeg, bake further 15 minutes or until custard is just set, cool. Refrigerate until cold.

Custard: Whisk eggs, essence and sugar in bowl until combined. Heat milk until hot, quickly whisk into egg mixture.

Serves 6 to 8.
- Recipe can be made a day ahead.
- Storage: Covered, in refrigerator.
- Freeze: Not suitable.
- Microwave: Not suitable.

Damper

In the early colonial days of Australia, there was no yeast, and the first settlers lacked the knowledge to make a substitute, so they made damper, an unleavened bread cooked in the ashes of a camp fire or open fireplace. Traditionally, damper consists of flour and water and a good pinch of salt. We've enriched this damper with butter and some milk; we leave the choice of salt to the cook.

3 cups self-raising flour
30g butter
½ cup milk
1 cup water, approximately

Sift flour into bowl, rub in butter. Make well in centre, add milk and enough water to mix to a soft sticky dough. Use a knife for best results.

Turn dough onto lightly floured surface; knead lightly until smooth. Press into 15cm circle, place on greased oven tray. Cut a cross through the dough, about 1cm deep. Brush dough with a little extra milk or water, then dust with a little extra flour. Bake in moderately hot oven about 30 minutes or until damper sounds hollow when tapped. Break damper open, serve pieces hot with butter and golden syrup, jam or honey.

■ Recipe best made just before serving.
■ Freeze: Suitable.
■ Microwave: Not suitable.

Date and Walnut Rolls

There are several types and sizes of nut roll tins available. Some open in the middle, some have holes in the lids to allow steam to escape. Only ever half fill the nut roll tins with mixture. Be careful of hot steam when turning out the cooked rolls.

1 cup (180g) chopped dates
60g butter
1 cup brown sugar, firmly packed
1 cup water
½ teaspoon bicarbonate of soda
1 egg, lightly beaten
½ cup chopped walnuts
2 cups self-raising flour

Grease 2 x 8cm x 17cm nut roll tins.

Combine dates, butter, sugar and water in pan, stir over heat, without boiling, until sugar is dissolved. Bring to boil, remove from heat; cool.

Stir soda, egg, nuts and sifted flour into date mixture. Spoon mixture evenly into prepared tins, replace lids. Bake, standing upright, in moderate oven about 40 minutes. Stand rolls 10 minutes before removing lids and turning onto wire rack to cool. Serve sliced with butter.

■ Recipe can be made 2 days ahead.
■ Storage: Airtight container.
■ Freeze: Suitable.
■ Microwave: Not suitable.

LEFT: Damper.
RIGHT: Date and Walnut Rolls.

Date Pudding

3 cups (500g) dates, chopped
90g butter
¾ cup brown sugar, firmly packed
¾ cup water
1 tablespoon brown malt vinegar
2 eggs, lightly beaten
1 tablespoon brandy
2 cups plain flour
½ cup self-raising flour
1 teaspoon bicarbonate of soda
1 teaspoon ground cinnamon
1 teaspoon mixed spice
½ cup milk

Grease aluminium pudding steamer (8 cup capacity). Combine dates, butter, sugar and water in pan, stir over heat, without boiling, until butter is melted and sugar dissolved; bring to boil, reduce heat, simmer, uncovered, 5 minutes. Stir in vinegar; cool to room temperature.

Stir eggs and brandy into date mixture, then stir in sifted dry ingredients and milk in 2 batches.

Spoon mixture into prepared steamer, cover steamer with greased foil, secure with string or lid. Place steamer in large pan with enough boiling water to come halfway up side of steamer; boil, covered, about 2½ hours. Replenish water when necessary. Serve pudding warm with custard or cream.
Serves 8 to 10.
■ Recipe can be made 4 days ahead.
■ Storage: Covered, in refrigerator.
■ Freeze: Suitable.
■ Microwave: Not suitable.

Devil's Food Cake

180g butter
1¾ cups caster sugar
3 eggs
1½ cups self-raising flour
½ cup plain flour
½ teaspoon bicarbonate of soda
⅔ cup cocoa
3 teaspoons dry instant coffee
½ teaspoon red food colouring
½ cup water
½ cup milk

RICH CHOCOLATE FROSTING
60g dark chocolate
60g unsalted butter

Grease 2 deep 20cm round cake pans, line bases with paper, grease paper. Beat butter and sugar in small bowl with electric mixer until light and fluffy, add eggs, 1 at a time, beating well between additions.

Transfer mixture to large bowl, fold in sifted flours, soda and cocoa with combined coffee, colouring, water and milk, in 2 batches. Pour into prepared pans, bake in moderate oven about 45 minutes. Turn cakes onto wire rack to cool.

Join cold cakes with whipped or mock cream, top with rich chocolate frosting.
Rich Chocolate Frosting: Combine chocolate and butter in heatproof bowl over pan of simmering water, stir until smooth. Remove from heat. Cool at room temperature until spreadable, stir occasionally while cooling.
■ Uniced cake can be made 2 days ahead.
■ Storage: Airtight container.
■ Freeze: Uniced cake suitable.
■ Microwave: Icing suitable.

RIGHT: From top: Diplomat Pudding, Date Pudding.
FAR RIGHT: Devil's Food Cake.

Diplomat Pudding

An old and popular dessert; other names for this include Cabinet Pudding, Charter Pudding,
Chancellor's Pudding or Newcastle Pudding. It is often very rich, but this is a simpler version.

2 tablespoons stale breadcrumbs
11 thin white slices of bread
1 cup milk
⅓ cup blanched almonds, chopped
⅓ cup currants
⅓ cup sultanas
2 tablespoons cornflour
150g butter
2 teaspoons vanilla essence
1 cup caster sugar
4 eggs, separated

Grease aluminium pudding steamer (6 cup capacity), sprinkle inside with the breadcrumbs. Discard crusts from bread slices, cut bread into small cubes, place in large bowl. Place milk in pan, bring to boil, pour over bread, cover, stand 30 minutes. Beat softened bread mixture with wooden spoon until smooth, stir in nuts, fruit and cornflour.

Beat butter, essence and sugar in small bowl with electric mixer until light and fluffy, beat in yolks. Stir butter mixture into bread mixture. Beat egg whites in small bowl with electric mixer until soft peaks form, fold into bread

mixture in 2 batches. Spoon mixture into prepared steamer, cover steamer with greased foil, secure with string or lid.

Place steamer in large pan with enough boiling water to come halfway up side of steamer; boil, covered, for about 2 hours. Replenish water when necessary. Serve warm with custard or cream.

Serves 6 to 8.

■ Recipe can be made 3 days ahead.
■ Storage: Covered, in refrigerator.
■ Freezer: Suitable.
■ Microwave: Not suitable.

Dundee Cake

180g butter, softened
¾ cup caster sugar
5 eggs, lightly beaten
1½ cups plain flour
½ cup self-raising flour
½ teaspoon mixed spice
⅓ cup milk
1¼ cups (250g) raisins, chopped
1½ cups (250g) currants
1¼ cups (250g) sultanas
2 tablespoons mixed peel
⅓ cup glace cherries, chopped
2 tablespoons blanched almonds
red glace cherries, extra
blanched almonds, extra
1 tablespoon brandy

Line deep 20cm round cake pan with 3 layers of baking paper, bringing paper 5cm above edge of pan.

Beat butter, sugar, eggs, sifted dry ingredients and milk in large bowl with electric mixer on medium speed for about 3 minutes or until mixture changes colour slightly. Stir in fruit and nuts, mix well.

Spread mixture into prepared pan, decorate top with extra cherries and nuts. Bake in a slow oven about 3 hours.

Brush hot cake with brandy; cover with foil, cool in pan.

■ Recipe can be made a week ahead.
■ Storage: Airtight container.
■ Freeze: Suitable
■ Microwave: Not suitable.

BELOW: Dundee Cake
RIGHT: From top: Easter Biscuits, Eccles Cakes.

Easter Biscuits

An early English recipe for Easter Cakes is almost exactly the same as this, but we know them as biscuits.

2 cups plain flour
150g butter
½ cup caster sugar
¼ cup currants
½ teaspoon grated lemon rind
1 egg, lightly beaten
caster sugar, extra

Sift flour into bowl; rub in butter. Stir in sugar, currants, rind and egg; mix to a firm dough. Roll dough to 5mm thickness, cut into 5cm rounds, place about 3cm apart on lightly greased oven trays. Bake in moderate oven about 15 minutes or until lightly coloured. While still hot, sprinkle with a little extra sugar, cool on trays.
Makes about 50.
■ Recipe can be made a week ahead.
■ Storage: Airtight container.
■ Freeze: Suitable.
■ Microwave: Not suitable.

Eccles Cakes

It is thought the Crusaders introduced these to England when they returned from the Holy Land in the 13th century.

3 sheets ready-rolled puff pastry
1 egg yolk
caster sugar

FILLING
30g butter
¾ cup currants
¼ cup chopped mixed peel
2 tablespoons caster sugar
½ teaspoon ground nutmeg
½ teaspoon mixed spice

Cut pastry into 11cm rounds. Place a level tablespoon of filling in centre of each round. Pinch edges together to enclose filling. Turn smooth side up onto lightly floured surface, flatten gently with rolling pin so currants just show through pastry. Shape into ovals, place on greased oven trays. Brush with egg yolk, sprinkle lightly with sugar, cut 3 small slits in tops of each oval. Bake in moderately hot oven about 15 minutes or until browned.
Filling: Combine butter, fruit, sugar and spices in pan, stir over low heat until butter is melted; cool.
Makes 12.
■ Recipe can be made 2 days ahead.
■ Storage: Airtight container.
■ Freeze: Suitable.
■ Microwave: Filling suitable.

Fairy Bread

This is a modern name for 'hundreds and thousands', traditionally served on bread and butter at children's parties.

4 slices of white bread
15g butter, softened
**2 tablespoons hundreds and
    thousands**

Discard crusts from bread, spread each slice with butter. Sprinkle with hundreds and thousands; cut into 4 triangles. Makes 16.
■ Recipe can be made 3 hours ahead.
■ Storage: Covered, in refrigerator.
■ Freeze: Not suitable.

Fairy Cakes

To make Butterfly Cakes, a variation of Fairy Cakes, cut the circle of cut-out cake in half, replace on the cream like wings. Decorate with silver cachous.
1½ cups self-raising flour
⅔ cup caster sugar
125g butter, softened
3 eggs
¼ cup milk
1 teaspoon vanilla essence
**½ cup jam or lemon butter,
    approximately**
300ml carton thickened cream

Line 2 x 12 hole deep patty pans with paper cases.

Sift dry ingredients into small bowl of electric mixer, add butter, eggs, milk and essence. Beat on medium speed about 3 minutes or until mixture is smooth and slightly lighter in colour. Drop 1½ tablespoons of mixture into prepared paper cases. Bake in moderate oven about 20 minutes or until lightly browned; cool in pans.

Using a fine pointed knife, cut circles from tops of cakes about 1cm from edge and about 1½cm down into patty cakes.

Place about ½ teaspoon of jam or lemon butter into cavities of cakes, top with whipped cream. Place tops into position. Dust with icing sugar.
Makes 24.
■ Recipe can be prepared a day ahead.
■ Storage: Unfilled cakes in airtight container. Filled cakes, covered, in refrigerator.
■ Freeze: Unfilled cakes suitable.
■ Microwave. Not suitable.

Finger Buns

2 x 7g sachets granulated yeast
¼ cup caster sugar
1½ cups warm milk
4 cups plain flour
60g butter
1 egg, lightly beaten
½ cup sultanas
¼ cup currants
¼ cup coconut
GLAZE
1 tablespoon caster sugar
1 teaspoon gelatine
1 tablespoon hot water
ICING
1 cup icing sugar
10g butter, melted
1 tablespoon milk, approximately
pink food colouring

Grease 2 x 20cm x 30cm lamington pans.

Combine yeast, sugar and milk in small bowl. Cover, stand in warm place about 10 minutes or until mixture is frothy.

Sift flour into large bowl, rub in butter. Stir in yeast mixture, egg and fruit, mix to a soft dough. Cover bowl, stand in warm place about 45 minutes or until dough is doubled in size.

Turn dough onto lightly floured surface, knead about 5 minutes or until smooth. Divide dough into 16 pieces, knead into buns 15cm long. Place buns into prepared pans, cover loosely with lightly oiled plastic wrap, stand in warm place about 10 minutes or until buns are well risen.

Bake buns in hot oven about 8 minutes, cover loosely with foil, bake about further 5 minutes. Turn buns onto wire rack, brush with glaze, cool.

Spread icing along tops of buns; sprinkle with coconut.
Glaze: Combine all ingredients in small pan, stir over heat, without boiling, until sugar and gelatine have dissolved.
Icing: Sift icing sugar into bowl, stir in butter and enough milk to make a stiff paste; tint pink with colouring. Stir over hot water until spreadable.
Makes 16.
■ Buns can be made a day ahead.
■ Storage: Airtight container.
■ Freeze: Uncooked buns suitable.
■ Microwave: Glaze suitable.

Right: Clockwise from right: Fairy Bread, Fairy and Butterfly Cakes, Finger Buns.

Cabinet and wooden horse from Woollahra Galleries.

Flapjacks

(American)

The American style flapjacks, also known as sweet oatcakes or griddle cakes, are a bit like king-sized, slightly softer and lighter pikelets.

1 cup self-raising flour
½ teaspoon baking powder
1 tablespoon caster sugar
1 egg, lightly beaten
1 cup milk
30g butter, melted
30g butter, extra
WHIPPED BUTTER
100g butter

Sift flour, baking powder and sugar into medium bowl. Stir in egg, milk and melted butter (or blend or process these ingredients until smooth).

Heat heavy-based pan, grease lightly with some of the extra butter; pour ¼ cup of batter into pan, cook about 2 minutes or until lightly browned. Turn, cook other side until browned. Repeat with remaining batter and extra butter. Serve flapjacks hot with maple syrup and whipped butter or ice-cream.

Whipped Butter: Beat butter in small bowl with electric mixer until fluffy.

Makes about 8.

■ Recipe best made just before serving.
■ Freeze: Not suitable.
■ Microwave: Not suitable.

Flapjacks

(British)

It is important to use the traditional (not the quick cook) oats in this recipe to get the correct texture.

90g butter
5 tablespoons demerara sugar
1⅓ cups (120g) rolled oats

Grease a 20cm round sandwich pan, line base with paper, grease paper.

Cream butter and sugar in small bowl with electric mixer until light and fluffy; stir in oats. Press mixture into prepared pan; bake in moderately hot oven about 20 minutes, or until lightly browned. Cool 5 minutes in pan, mark into wedges with knife, loosen edges; cool in pan.

■ Recipe can be made 3 days ahead.
■ Storage: Airtight container.
■ Freeze: Suitable.
■ Microwave: Not suitable.

Florentines

¾ cup sultanas
2 cups (60g) Corn Flakes
¾ cup unsalted roasted peanuts, chopped
½ cup chopped red glace cherries
⅔ cup sweetened condensed milk
150g dark chocolate, melted

Combine sultanas, Corn Flakes, peanuts, cherries and milk in bowl; mix well. Place 1½ tablespoons of mixture on oven trays covered with baking paper. Bake in moderate oven about 10 minutes or until lightly browned; cool on trays.

Spread base of each biscuit with chocolate. Make wavy lines in chocolate with fork just before chocolate sets.

Makes about 18.

■ Recipe can be made a month ahead.
■ Storage: Covered, in refrigerator.
■ Freeze: Suitable.
■ Microwave: Chocolate suitable.

LEFT: From front: Flapjacks (American), Flapjacks (British).
ABOVE: Florentines.

51

Fruit Mince Pies

No traditional Christmas feast would be complete without a batch of these delicious, festive treats.

Fruit mince is available in jars, or you can make your own.

2 cups (300g) plain flour
2 tablespoons packaged ground almonds
180g butter
1 teaspoon grated lemon rind
¼ cup icing sugar
1 egg yolk
¼ cup milk, approximately
2 cups (500g) fruit mince
1 egg, lightly beaten
icing sugar

FRUIT MINCE
1 small apple, peeled, cored
½ cup sultanas
⅓ cup mixed peel
2 tablespoons glace cherries, chopped
⅓ cup currants
⅓ cup blanched almonds, chopped
1 cup (200g) brown sugar, firmly packed
½ teaspoon grated lemon rind
1 tablespoon lemon juice
½ teaspoon grated orange rind
½ teaspoon ground cinnamon
½ teaspoon mixed spice
¼ teaspoon ground nutmeg
40g butter, melted
2 tablespoons brandy

Lightly grease 2 x 12 hole shallow patty pans. Sift flour into bowl, stir in almonds, rub in butter, then stir in rind and sifted icing sugar. Stir in yolk and enough milk to make ingredients cling together. Knead dough on lightly floured surface until smooth, cover, refrigerate 30 minutes.

Roll pastry until 3mm thick. Cut out 7½cm rounds, place into patty pans. Drop tablespoons of fruit mince into each pastry case. Roll scraps of pastry on lightly floured surface, cut out desired shapes. Brush each pastry shape with egg, place egg side down on fruit mince. Bake in moderately hot oven about 20 minutes, or until lightly browned. Dust with a little sifted icing sugar before serving.

Fruit Mince: Finely chop apple and half the sultanas, combine in bowl with remaining sultanas and remaining ingredients; mix well. Transfer mixture to sterilised jar. Store in refrigerator for at least 3 days before using. Makes about 2 cups fruit mince.

Makes 24.

■ Pies can be made a week ahead.
■ Storage: Airtight container.
■ Freeze: 3 months.
■ Microwave: Not suitable.

BELOW: Fruit Mince Pies.
RIGHT: Garibaldi Slice.

Below: China from Wedgwood; fabric from Redelman & Son.

Garibaldi Slice

These biscuits were unkindly called 'squashed flys' by children. This was probably due to the appearance and slightly acid flavour of the filling.

½ cup currants
½ cup raisins
1½ cups (240g) sultanas
3 cups plain flour
250g butter, chopped
⅓ cup caster sugar
2 egg yolks
2 tablespoons water, approximately
caster sugar, extra

Grease 26cm x 32cm Swiss roll pan. Blend or process fruit until chopped.

Sift flour into bowl, rub in butter, stir in sugar. Add yolks and enough water to mix to a soft dough. Turn dough onto lightly floured surface, knead lightly until smooth; cover, refrigerate 30 minutes.

Divide pastry in half; roll 1 portion between sheets of greaseproof paper large enough to fit base of prepared pan. Spread with fruit; cover with remaining pastry, press all over with hand to join slice; trim edges. Score into rectangles through top layer of pastry; brush with a little water, sprinkle with a little extra sugar; prick with fork. Bake in moderately hot oven 10 minutes; reduce heat to moderate, bake about further 30 minutes or until browned. Cut slice while hot; cool in pan.

■ Recipe can be made a week ahead.
■ Storage: Airtight container.
■ Freeze: Suitable.
■ Microwave: Not suitable.

Gem Scones

Old-fashioned cast gem irons are available from specialty cookware shops, or even second-hand shops.

40g butter
⅓ cup caster sugar
1 egg, lightly beaten
1½ cups self-raising flour
1 cup milk

Place 2 ungreased 12 hole gem irons into hot oven.

Beat butter and sugar in small bowl with electric mixer until light and fluffy; add egg gradually, beat until combined. Stir in sifted flour and milk in 2 batches.

Lightly grease hot gem irons, drop level tablespoons of mixture into each hole. Bake in hot oven about 10 minutes or until lightly browned. Serve hot with butter or jam and cream. Makes about 24.

Note: To make jelly cakes (see page 64) from this recipe, place mixture into cold greased gem irons to prevent peaks forming during cooking.

▪ Recipe best made just before serving.
▪ Freeze: Suitable.
▪ Microwave: Not suitable.

Gingerbread

Ginger, which is a native of Asia, was first used in Western Europe more than 2000 years ago. Other Asian spices, such as cardamom, cinnamon and black pepper, were also imported around that time. Gingerbread is thought to be one of the world's earliest sweet cakes.

1 cup golden syrup
1 cup water
⅔ cup brown sugar, firmly packed
250g butter
3½ cups plain flour
1 teaspoon bicarbonate of soda
2 tablespoons ground ginger
1 teaspoon ground nutmeg
1 teaspoon ground cinnamon

LEMON ICING
60g butter, softened
2 teaspoons grated lemon rind
2 tablespoons lemon juice
2 cups icing sugar

Grease 23cm square slab pan; line base with paper, grease paper.

Combine golden syrup, water, sugar and butter in large pan, stir over heat until butter is melted; bring to boil; remove from heat, cool to room temperature.

Stir sifted dry ingredients into butter mixture in two batches, beat gently until smooth. Pour mixture into prepared pan; bake in moderately slow oven about 1¼ hours. Stand cake 5 minutes before turning onto wire rack to cool. Spread cold cake with lemon icing.

Lemon Icing: Beat butter and rind in small bowl with wooden spoon, gradually beat in juice and sifted icing sugar.

▪ Recipe can be made a week ahead.
▪ Storage: Airtight container.
▪ Freeze: Suitable.
▪ Microwave: Not suitable.

LEFT: Gem Scones.
RIGHT: Clockwise from left: Gingerbread, Gingerbread Men, Gingernuts.

Left: Cabinet from Country Furniture Antiques; china from Mikasa; preserve jar and silver bowl from Woollahra Antiques.
Right: Gingerbread cutters available from The Bay Tree.

Gingerbread Men

By the 14th century, the most popular method of preparing gingerbread was to bake it in the shape of a 'man', and other shapes, such as animals.

Cutters of many shapes and sizes are available from specialty kitchen shops and department stores. The number of 'people' you will get from this batch of dough will depend on the size of the cutters used.

125g butter
½ cup brown sugar, firmly packed
½ cup golden syrup
1 egg yolk
2½ cups plain flour
1 tablespoon ground ginger
1 teaspoon bicarbonate of soda
ROYAL ICING
1 egg white
1½ cups pure icing sugar
food colouring

Cream butter and sugar in small bowl with electric mixer until light and fluffy, beat in golden syrup and yolk. Transfer mixture to large bowl, stir in sifted dry ingredients in 2 batches. Press mixture into a ball, knead on lightly floured surface until smooth; cover, refrigerate 30 minutes.

Roll dough between sheets of greaseproof paper to 4mm thickness. Cut gingerbread shapes from dough. Place shapes about 3cm apart on lightly greased oven trays. Bake in moderately hot oven about 8 minutes or until lightly browned and firm; cool on trays.

Spoon royal icing into piping bag fitted with a small plain tube, decorate shapes as desired.

Royal Icing: Whisk egg white in small bowl with a fork; gradually whisk in sifted icing sugar, about 1 tablespoon at a time, beat well between additions. Colour as desired. Keep bowl of icing covered with a damp cloth during use.

■ Recipe can be made 3 days ahead.
■ Storage: Airtight container.
■ Freeze: Uniced gingerbread suitable.
■ Microwave: Not suitable.

Gingernuts

Ginger has also long been used as a flavouring for biscuits. These deliciously crisp versions are sometimes known as ginger snaps.

90g butter
⅓ cup brown sugar
⅓ cup golden syrup
1⅓ cups plain flour
¾ teaspoon bicarbonate of soda
1 teaspoon ground cinnamon
1 tablespoon ground ginger
¼ teaspoon ground cloves

Combine butter, sugar and golden syrup in pan, stir over heat until butter is melted. Remove from heat, stir in sifted dry ingredients; stand until mixture feels warm to the touch.

Roll 2 level teaspoons of mixture into balls, place on greased oven trays, about 3cm apart; flatten slightly. Bake in moderate oven about 12 minutes or until browned. Loosen biscuits; cool on trays.
Makes about 35.
■ Recipe can be made a week ahead.
■ Storage: Airtight container.
■ Freeze: Suitable.
■ Microwave: Not suitable.

Ginger Pudding

Ginger, like cinnamon, cloves and a number of other spices native to Asia, lends itself equally well to sweet or savoury dishes. This delicious pudding has long been a favourite.

180g butter
½ cup brown sugar, firmly packed
½ cup golden syrup
¼ cup honey
¼ cup water
2 eggs, lightly beaten
1½ cups plain flour
1½ cups self-raising flour
1½ tablespoons ground ginger
1 teaspoon bicarbonate of soda
2 tablespoons finely chopped glace ginger

Lightly grease aluminium pudding steamer (6 cup capacity), line base with paper, grease paper.

Combine butter, sugar, golden syrup, honey and water in pan; stir over heat until butter is melted. Bring to boil, remove from heat; cool to room temperature.

Stir eggs into butter mixture, then sifted dry ingredients and glace ginger; mix well. Spoon mixture into prepared steamer, cover with greased foil, secure with string or lid. Place steamer in boiler with enough boiling water to come halfway up side of steamer; boil, covered, for about 2 hours or until firm. Replenish water when necessary. Serve pudding hot with custard, cream or ice-cream, if desired.
Serves 6 to 8.
■ Recipe can be made a day ahead.
■ Storage: Covered, in refrigerator.
■ Freeze: Suitable.
■ Microwave: Not suitable.

Ginger Sponge

5 eggs, separated
¾ cup caster sugar
1 tablespoon golden syrup
⅓ cup self-raising flour
⅓ cup cornflour
3 teaspoons ground ginger
1 teaspoon ground cinnamon
2 teaspoons cocoa
¾ cup thickened cream

Grease 2 deep 20cm round cake pans.

Beat egg whites in medium bowl with electric mixer until soft peaks form; gradually add sugar, beat until dissolved between additions. Beat in egg yolks and golden syrup. Triple sift dry ingredients, fold into mixture. Divide mixture evenly between prepared pans. Bake in moderately hot oven about 18 minutes. Turn sponges immediately onto wire racks to cool.

Beat cream until soft peaks form, join cakes with cream. Dust top with a little sifted icing sugar, if desired.
■ Recipe best made on day of serving.
■ Storage: Covered, in refrigerator.
■ Freeze: Unfilled cake suitable.
■ Microwave: Not suitable.

LEFT: Ginger Pudding.
RIGHT: Ginger Sponge.

Left: China from Wedgewood; glass from Bohemia Crystal; fabric from Redelmen & Son.

Golden Syrup Dumplings

Although less common now, golden syrup, which is derived from cane sugar juice, was once a much loved staple of children and adults alike.

1¼ cups self-raising flour
30g butter
⅓ cup golden syrup
⅓ cup milk

SAUCE
30g butter
¾ cup brown sugar, firmly packed
½ cup golden syrup
1⅔ cups water

Sift flour into bowl, rub in butter, gradually stir in golden syrup and milk. Drop tablespoonsful of mixture into simmering sauce; simmer, covered, about 20 minutes or until dumplings are cooked through. Serve with sauce, topped with cream or ice-cream, if desired.

Sauce: Combine all ingredients in medium pan (base should be about 18cm wide); stir over heat, without boiling, until sugar is dissolved. Bring to the boil, without stirring, reduce to simmer.

Serves 4 to 6.

■ Recipe best made just before serving.
■ Freeze: Not suitable.
■ Microwave: Not suitable.

LEFT: Golden Syrup Dumplings.
ABOVE: From front: Honey Joys, Honey Jumbles.

Honey Jumbles

Over time there have been many versions of this very old British recipe. Originally called 'Jumbals', these biscuits were often made with a hole in the middle. This is our favourite, made with golden syrup.

They are best made a day before eating; overnight the flavour from the spices will develop and the texture will soften to a more cake-like consistency.

60g butter
½ cup brown sugar, firmly packed
¾ cup golden syrup
1 egg, lightly beaten
2½ cups plain flour
½ cup self-raising flour
½ teaspoon bicarbonate of soda
1 teaspoon ground cinnamon
½ teaspoon ground cloves
2 teaspoons ground ginger
1 teaspoon mixed spice

ICING
1 egg white
1½ cups icing sugar
2 teaspoons plain flour
1 tablespoon lemon juice,
**   approximately**
pink food colouring

Combine butter, sugar and golden syrup in medium pan, stir over low heat until sugar is dissolved and butter is melted; cool 10 minutes.

Transfer mixture to large bowl, stir in egg and sifted dry ingredients in 2 batches. Turn dough onto floured surface, knead gently until mixture loses its stickiness; cover, refrigerate 30 minutes.

Divide dough into 8 portions for easy management. Roll each portion into 2cm thick sausage, cut into 5 x 6cm lengths. Place onto greased oven trays, about 3cm apart. Round edges with lightly floured fingers, flatten gently with heel of hand. Bake in moderately slow oven about 12 minutes or until browned; cool on trays. Spread jumbles with pink and white icing.

Icing: Lightly beat egg white in small bowl, gradually stir in sifted icing sugar and flour. Stir in enough juice to make a spreadable consistency. Tint half the icing pink with colouring. Keep icing covered with a damp cloth while in use. Makes about 40.

■ Recipe best made a day ahead.
■ Storage: Uncovered, at room temperature.
■ Freeze: Uniced biscuits suitable.
■ Microwave: Not suitable.

Honey Joys

These are perennial bestsellers at school fetes, jumble sales and fund-raising stalls. Children seem to enjoy making them almost as much as eating them.

100g butter
¼ cup caster sugar
1 tablespoon honey
4 cups (120g) Corn Flakes

Line 2 x 12 hole deep patty pans with paper patty cases.

Combine butter, sugar and honey in pan, stir over heat, without boiling, until sugar is dissolved; bring to boil, remove from heat. Place Corn Flakes in large bowl, add honey mixture, stir gently to combine. Spoon mixture into paper cases, bake in moderate oven about 10 minutes.
Makes 24.

■ Recipe can be made a week ahead.
■ Storage: Airtight container.
■ Freeze: Not suitable.
■ Microwave: Butter mixture suitable.

Honey Roll

This delicious cream roll is a close copy of a commercial cake which has long been a popular staple of traditional cake shops. The origin of its name is rather mysterious as it is golden syrup, not honey, which gives the cake its special colour, texture and flavour.

60g butter
¾ cup golden syrup
¾ cup plain flour
½ cup self-raising flour
2 teaspoons ground ginger
1 teaspoon ground cinnamon
¾ teaspoon ground nutmeg
¼ teaspoon ground cloves
2 eggs
1 teaspoon bicarbonate of soda
¼ cup boiling water
½ cup coconut

WASHED MOCK CREAM
125g butter
1 teaspoon vanilla essence
1 tablespoon honey
½ cup caster sugar

Grease a 26cm x 32cm Swiss roll pan, line base and sides with paper; grease paper.

Beat butter in small bowl with electric mixer until smooth and creamy, gradually beat in golden syrup. Stir in sifted flours and spices, then stir in eggs. Quickly stir in combined soda and water. Spread mixture evenly into prepared pan, bake in moderate oven about 18 minutes.

Cover a wire rack with paper, sprinkle with coconut, turn cake onto coconut; carefully remove lining paper, loosely roll up cake from short side, using paper as a guide. Let stand for a few minutes, unroll, cool to room temperature.

Spread mock cream over cake, carefully re-roll cake.

Washed Mock Cream: Cream butter, essence, honey and sugar in small bowl with electric mixer until light and fluffy. Remove bowl from mixer, cover butter mixture with cold water, swirl water around bowl for 1 minute, pour off water. Return to mixer, beat mixture well. Repeat washing and beating until mixture is white in colour and sugar dissolved. You will need to do this about 6 times.

■ Recipe can be made a day ahead.
■ Storage: Covered, in refrigerator.
■ Freeze: Not suitable.
■ Microwave: Not suitable.

Hot Cross Buns

Although these delicious Easter treats are now traditionally served on Good Friday, in olden times they were thought to have holy powers and were present in many religious observances.

2 x 7g sachets granulated yeast
¼ cup caster sugar
1½ cups warm milk
4 cups plain flour
1 teaspoon mixed spice
½ teaspoon ground cinnamon
60g butter
1 egg
¾ cup sultanas

FLOUR PASTE FOR CROSSES
½ cup plain flour
2 teaspoons caster sugar
⅓ cup water, approximately

GLAZE
1 tablespoon caster sugar
1 teaspoon gelatine
1 tablespoon water

Combine yeast, sugar and milk in small bowl; cover, stand in warm place about 10 minutes or until mixture is frothy.

Sift flour and spices into large bowl, rub in butter. Stir in yeast mixture, egg and sultanas, mix to a soft sticky dough; cover, stand in warm place about 45 minutes or until dough is doubled in size.

Turn dough onto lightly floured surface, knead about 5 minutes or until smooth. Divide dough into 16 pieces, knead into balls; place balls into greased 23cm square slab pan; cover, stand in warm place about 10 minutes or until buns are risen to top of pan. Place flour paste for crosses in piping bag fitted with small plain tube, pipe crosses onto buns. Bake in hot oven about 20 minutes or until well browned. Turn buns onto wire rack, brush tops with hot glaze; cool on wire rack.

Flour Paste for Crosses: Combine flour and sugar in bowl. Gradually blend in enough water to form a smooth paste.

Glaze: Combine all ingredients in pan, stir over heat, without boiling, until sugar and gelatine are dissolved.

Makes 16.

■ Recipe can be made a day ahead.
■ Storage: Airtight container.
■ Freeze: Uncooked buns suitable.
■ Microwave: Glaze suitable.

LEFT: Honey Roll.
RIGHT: Hot Cross Buns.

Hummingbird Cake

A delectable American favourite, this moist cake is probably named after the brilliant tiny American hummingbirds, whose staple diet is nectar.

Keep cake in the refrigerator if weather is wet or humid.

1½ cups plain flour
1 cup caster sugar
½ teaspoon ground cinnamon
½ teaspoon bicarbonate of soda
3 eggs, lightly beaten
¾ cup oil
¾ cup chopped pecans or walnuts
2 cups mashed over-ripe bananas
½ cup undrained crushed pineapple in heavy syrup

CREAM CHEESE FROSTING

60g packaged cream cheese, softened
30g butter
1 teaspoon vanilla essence
1½ cups icing sugar

Lightly grease 23cm square slab pan, line base with paper, grease paper.

Sift flour, sugar, cinnamon and soda into large bowl. Stir in eggs, oil, nuts, banana and pineapple; stir until just combined. Pour mixture into prepared pan, bake in moderate oven about 1 hour. Stand cake 10 minutes before turning onto wire rack to cool. Spread cold cake with cream cheese frosting.

Cream Cheese Frosting: Beat cream cheese, butter and essence in small bowl with electric mixer until light and fluffy; gradually beat in sifted icing sugar.

■ Recipe can be made 3 days ahead.
■ Storage: Airtight container.
■ Freeze: Suitable.
■ Microwave: Not suitable.

Impossible Pie

Everyone loves a quick mix recipe. This one obligingly sorts itself out in the oven into 3 layers, hence its name.

½ **cup plain flour**
1 **cup caster sugar**
1 **cup (90g) coconut**
4 **eggs, lightly beaten**
2 **teaspoons vanilla essence**
125g **butter, melted**
2 **cups milk**

Lightly grease straight-sided 24cm pie dish. Sift flour into bowl, stir in sugar, coconut, eggs, essence, butter and milk. Pour into prepared pie dish, bake in moderate oven about 45 minutes or until lightly browned and set. Serve warm or cold with cream or fruit if desired.
Serves 6 to 8.

■ Recipe can be made a day ahead.
■ Storage: Covered, in refrigerator.
■ Freeze: Not suitable.
■ Microwave: Not suitable.

LEFT: Hummingbird Cake.
ABOVE: Impossible Pie.

Above: Plate from Villeroy & Boch; wooden tray and cloth from Belinda's Corner.

Jelly Cakes

These little jewels of cake, cream and jelly are made from gem scones. The old-fashioned cast gem irons are available from speciality cookware shops, or even second-hand shops.

85g packet strawberry jelly crystals
1 cup boiling water
1 cup cold water
½ cup thickened cream
1 tablespoon icing sugar
1½ cups (140g) coconut

GEM SCONES
40g butter
⅓ cup caster sugar
1 egg, lightly beaten
1½ cups self-raising flour
1 cup milk

Dissolve jelly crystals in boiling water, add cold water, refrigerate until partly set.

Trim rounded tops from gem scones, to give flat surface for joining scones.

Beat cream with sifted icing sugar in small bowl until soft peaks form. Sandwich scones with whipped cream. Place a scone on a slotted spoon or egg slide, spoon partly set jelly over the scone, roll carefully in coconut. Repeat with remaining scones and jelly. Refrigerate about 30 minutes or until jelly is set. Leftover jelly, cake trimmings and cream can be used to make trifle.

Gem Scones: Beat butter and sugar in small bowl with electric mixer until light and fluffy; add egg gradually, beat until combined. Stir in sifted flour and milk in 2 batches; stir until smooth.

Lightly grease 3 x 12 hole gem irons, drop 3 level teaspoons of mixture into each hole. Bake in hot oven about 8 minutes or until lightly browned. Turn onto wire rack to cool. Makes about 18.

■ Recipe can be made a day ahead.
■ Storage: Covered, in refrigerator.
■ Freeze: Not suitable.
■ Microwave: Not suitable.

ABOVE: Jelly Cakes.
RIGHT: Key Lime Pie.

Above: Tablecloth from Belinda's Corner. Right: China from Mikasa; lace tablecloth from Belinda's Corner; table from Country Form.

Key Lime Pie

The lime originally came from Asia, as did the other citrus fruits. The most common variety, the Key lime, flourishes in Florida, USA, where it's used in many dishes. There are lots of variations of this famous American recipe, but this one is our favourite.

1 cup plain flour
2 teaspoons icing sugar
60g butter
2 teaspoons lemon juice
1 tablespoon water, approximately

FILLING
¾ cup sweetened condensed milk
1 cup (200g) ricotta cheese
3 eggs, separated
2 teaspoons grated lemon rind
⅓ cup lime juice

Sift flour and icing sugar into bowl, rub in butter, stir in lemon juice and enough water to mix to a soft dough. Knead dough gently on lightly floured surface until smooth; cover, refrigerate 30 minutes.

Roll dough between sheets of greaseproof paper large enough to fit 23cm pie plate; ease into dish, trim edge. Line pastry with paper, fill with dried beans or rice. Bake in moderately hot oven 10 minutes. Remove paper and beans; bake about further 7 minutes or until lightly browned; cool.

Pour filling into pastry case; bake in moderate oven about 25 minutes or until filling is set; cool.

Refrigerate pie until cold; dust with sifted icing sugar just before serving.

Filling: Blend or process milk, cheese, egg yolks, rind and juice until smooth; transfer to large bowl. Beat egg whites in small bowl until soft peaks form, fold into lime mixture in 2 batches.

Serves 6 to 8.
■ Recipe best made a day ahead.
■ Storage: Covered, in refrigerator.
■ Freeze: Not suitable.
■ Microwave: Not suitable.

Kisses

Now used to describe a variety of one-bite sweet delicacies, the name probably derives from the days when bread was home-baked. Any little curly bits of crust which formed as the bread cooled were broken off and eagerly eaten by children. This treat was known as 'kissing crust'.

125g butter
½ cup caster sugar
1 egg
⅓ cup plain flour
¼ cup self-raising flour
⅔ cup cornflour
¼ cup custard powder

VIENNA CREAM
60g butter
¾ cup icing sugar
2 teaspoons milk

Beat butter and sugar in small bowl with electric mixer until smooth and creamy; add egg, beat only until combined. Stir in sifted dry ingredients in 2 batches. Spoon mixture into piping bag fitted with 1cm fluted tube. Pipe 3cm rosettes of mixture about 3cm apart onto lightly greased oven trays. Bake in moderately hot oven about 10 minutes or until lightly browned. Loosen biscuits, cool on trays.

Sandwich cold biscuits with Vienna Cream; dust with a little extra sifted icing sugar, if desired.

Vienna Cream: Beat butter until white as possible, gradually beat in half the sifted icing sugar, then milk; gradually beat in remaining icing sugar.
Makes about 40.
■ Recipe can be made 3 days ahead.
■ Storage: Airtight container.
■ Freeze: Unfilled kisses suitable.
■ Microwave: Not suitable.

Lamingtons

Lamingtons, the staple of all good fetes and fund-raising enterprises, are said to be named after Lord Lamington, Governor of Queensland from 1895 to 1901.

The cake is easy to handle if it is a little stale; day old cake is ideal. Sponge or butter cake can be used. Lamingtons can be filled with jam and cream, if desired.

6 eggs
⅔ cup caster sugar
⅓ cup cornflour
½ cup plain flour
⅓ cup self-raising flour
2 cups (180g) coconut,
  approximately

ICING
4 cups (500g) icing sugar
½ cup cocoa
15g butter, melted
⅔ cup milk

Grease 23cm square slab pan. Beat eggs in medium bowl with electric mixer about 10 minutes, or until thick and creamy. Gradually beat in sugar, dissolving between additions. Fold in triple-sifted flours. Spread mixture into prepared pan. Bake in moderate oven about 30 minutes. Turn onto wire rack to cool.

Cut cake into 16 squares, dip squares into icing, drain off excess icing, toss squares in coconut. Place lamingtons on wire rack to set.
Icing: Sift icing sugar and cocoa into heatproof bowl, stir in butter and milk. Stir over pan of simmering water until icing is of coating consistency.
Makes 16.
■ Cake best made a day ahead.
■ Storage: Airtight container.
■ Freeze: Suitable.
■ Microwave: Not suitable.

RIGHT: Kisses.
LEFT: Lamingtons.

Right: Silver tray and sugar bowl from Whitehill Silver & Plate; tablecloth from Belinda's Corner.

Lardy Cake

This delicious flaky yeast cake originated in a number of English counties, such as Wiltshire and Sussex, where pigs were raised. Dough left over from making bread would be rolled with lard, sugar and currants for a baking day treat.

15g compressed yeast
1 teaspoon caster sugar
¾ cup warm milk
2 cups plain flour
pinch salt
1 egg, lightly beaten
¼ cup currants
125g lard
⅓ cup caster sugar, extra
2 teaspoons oil
1 tablespoon crystal sugar

Cream yeast with caster sugar in small bowl; stir in milk, cover, stand in warm place about 15 minutes or until frothy. Grease deep 20 cm round cake pan.

Sift flour and salt into large bowl, stir in yeast mixture, egg and currants; mix to soft dough. Turn dough onto floured surface, knead about 3 minutes or until dough is smooth and elastic.

Roll dough to about 15cm x 30cm rectangle, spread half the lard over two-thirds of the dough, sprinkle with half the extra caster sugar. Fold the unlarded third of the dough over. Fold the top third of the dough over, turn dough halfway round, open end towards you. Roll out dough and fold again using the remaining lard and extra caster sugar. Then roll and fold twice more, without lard and sugar.

Shape dough into a round by turning ends under, place into prepared pan, press dough to fit pan. Brush top with oil, sprinkle with the crystal sugar. Stand, uncovered, in warm place about 45 minutes, or until dough is well risen. Slash top of cake with a sharp knife in crisscross fashion. Bake in moderately hot oven 40 minutes or until cake is well browned. Turn onto wire rack. Serve warm with butter.

■ Recipe best made just before serving.
■ Freeze: Not suitable.
■ Microwave: Not suitable.

Lemon Cheesecake

Cheesecake was very popular in ancient Greece and it was probably the Romans, after their conquest of Greece, who introduced this delight to Western Europe. Lemon cheesecake, which appeared in English cookbooks as early as 1747, may have been responsible for converting most Australians to the delights of cheesecake in all its variations.

250g packet plain sweet biscuits
125g butter, melted

FILLING
250g packet cream cheese, softened
400g can sweetened condensed milk
2 teaspoons grated lemon rind
⅓ cup lemon juice
1 teaspoon gelatine
1 tablespoon water

Lemon Chiffon Pie

The French word chiffon is applied to materials, such as fabric and food, which are light, soft and silky. It is perfect to describe the texture of this popular dessert.

**1¾ cups (180g) plain sweet
    biscuit crumbs**
125g butter, melted
FILLING
4 eggs, separated
⅓ cup caster sugar
3 teaspoons gelatine
2 teaspoons grated lemon rind
⅓ cup lemon juice
⅓ cup water
⅓ cup caster sugar, extra

Combine biscuit crumbs and butter in bowl, mix well. Press firmly over base and side of 23cm pie plate; refrigerate 30 minutes or until firm.

Spread filling into crumb crust, refrigerate several hours or until set.

Filling: Combine egg yolks, caster sugar, gelatine, rind, juice and water in heatproof bowl. Stir over simmering water until mixture has thickened slightly. Remove from heat, pour into large bowl, cover, cool to room temperature. Mixture should be set to about the consistency of unbeaten egg white before adding remaining ingredients.

Beat egg whites in small bowl with electric mixer until soft peaks form, add extra sugar gradually, beat until dissolved between additions; fold through lemon mixture in 2 batches. Serves 6 to 8.

■ Recipe can be made a day ahead.
■ Storage: Covered, in refrigerator.
■ Freeze: Not suitable.
■ Microwave: Not suitable.

Lightly grease 20cm springform tin. Blend, process or crush biscuits finely; stir in butter. Using a flat-bottomed glass press mixture evenly over base and side of prepared tin. Refrigerate crumb crust 30 minutes or until firm.

Pour filling into crumb crust; refrigerate several hours or until set. Decorate with whipped cream, strawberries and lemon rind, if desired.

Filling: Beat cream cheese in small bowl with electric mixer until smooth, beat in condensed milk, rind and juice; beat until smooth. Soften gelatine in water in cup, stir over hot water until dissolved. Stir gelatine mixture into lemon mixture.

Serves 6 to 8.

■ Recipe best made a day before
    serving.
■ Storage: Covered, in refrigerator.
■ Freeze: Not suitable.
■ Microwave: Gelatine suitable.

LEFT: Lardy Cake.
ABOVE: Lemon Cheesecake.
RIGHT: Lemon Chiffon Pie.

Lemon Delicious

Originally an English pudding, this dish is sometimes called baked lemon pudding. There are now many variations. Interestingly, the Australian version has had its name shortened, probably as a time-honoured mark of affection.

3 eggs, separated
½ cup caster sugar
30g butter, melted
1 cup milk
2 teaspoons grated lemon rind
⅓ cup lemon juice
½ cup self-raising flour
½ cup caster sugar, extra

Beat egg yolks and sugar in small bowl with electric mixer until thick and creamy; transfer to large bowl. Stir in butter, milk, rind, juice and sifted flour.

Beat egg whites in small bowl with electric mixer until soft peaks form, add extra sugar gradually, beat until dissolved between additions. Fold into lemon mixture in 2 batches. Pour into lightly greased ovenproof dish (6 cup capacity), or 6 individual dishes (1 cup capacity). Place in baking dish with enough hot water to come halfway up side of dish. Bake in moderate oven about 50 minutes (about 30 minutes for individual dishes) or until pudding is set.
Serves 6.
■ Recipe best made just before serving.
■ Freeze: Not suitable.
■ Microwave: Not suitable.

Lemon Meringue Pie

The meringue is believed to have been invented by a Swiss pastry-cook called Gasparini in 1720. It quickly became a favourite of the French court and Marie-Antoinette was apparently so fond of it that she used to make it with her own regal hands!

1½ cups plain flour
3 teaspoons icing sugar
140g butter
1 egg yolk, lightly beaten
2 tablespoons water, approximately

FILLING
½ cup cornflour
1 cup caster sugar
½ cup lemon juice
1¼ cups water
2 teaspoons grated lemon rind
3 egg yolks
60g unsalted butter

MERINGUE
3 egg whites
½ cup caster sugar

Lightly grease 24cm flan tin.

Sift flour and icing sugar into bowl, rub in butter. Add yolk and enough water to make ingredients cling together. Press dough into ball, knead gently on lightly floured surface until smooth; cover, refrigerate 30 minutes.

Roll dough on lightly floured surface large enough to line prepared tin; trim edges. Place tin on oven tray, line pastry with paper, fill with dried beans or rice. Bake in a moderately hot oven 10 minutes, remove paper and beans, bake further 10 minutes or until pastry is lightly browned; cool to room temperature.

Spread filling into pastry case, top with meringue. Bake in a moderate oven about 5 minutes or until meringue is lightly browned. Stand 5 minutes before serving.

Filling: Combine cornflour and sugar in pan, gradually stir in juice and water, stir until smooth. Stir over heat until mixture boils and thickens (mixture should be very thick). Reduce heat, simmer, stirring 30 seconds. Remove from heat, quickly stir in rind, yolks and butter, stir until butter is melted; cover, cool to room temperature.

Meringue: Beat egg whites in small bowl with electric mixer until soft peaks form, gradually add sugar, beat until dissolved between additions.
Serves 6 to 8.
■ Recipe can be made a day ahead.
■ Storage: Covered, in refrigerator.
■ Freeze: Not suitable.
■ Microwave: Not suitable.

LEFT: Lemon Delicious.
RIGHT: Lemon Meringue Pie.

Right: China from Villeroy & Boch.

Lumberjack Cake

**2 large (400g) apples, finely
    chopped**
1 cup (200g) chopped dates
1 teaspoon bicarbonate of soda
1 cup boiling water
125g butter
1 teaspoon vanilla essence
1 cup sugar
1 egg
1½ cups plain flour

TOPPING
60g butter
½ cup brown sugar, firmly packed
½ cup milk
⅔ cup shredded coconut

Grease deep 19cm square cake pan, line base with paper, grease paper. Combine apples, dates, soda and water in bowl, cover, stand until warm.

Beat butter, essence and sugar in small bowl with electric mixer until light and creamy, add egg, beat until combined. Transfer mixture to large bowl, stir in sifted flour alternately with apple mixture, pour into prepared pan. Bake in moderate oven 50 minutes, spread with topping, bake about further 30 minutes, or until topping is golden brown. Cool cake in pan.

Topping: Combine butter, sugar, milk and coconut in pan, stir over low heat until butter is melted and sugar dissolved.

■ Recipe can be made a week ahead.
■ Storage: Covered, in refrigerator.
■ Freeze: Suitable.
■ Microwave: Not suitable.

*BELOW: Lumberjack Cake.
RIGHT: Macaroons: Almond, Coconut.*

Macaroons, Almond

*From an old French recipe. The Italian
versions are called amaretti.*

2 egg whites
½ cup caster sugar
**1¼ cups (125g) packaged ground
    almonds**
½ teaspoon almond essence
2 tablespoons plain flour
2 tablespoons flaked almonds

Beat egg whites in small bowl with electric mixer until soft peaks form, add sugar gradually, beating until dissolved between additions. Fold in ground almonds, essence and sifted flour in 2 batches.

Line oven trays with baking paper. Drop level tablespoons of mixture onto trays about 5cm apart. Place a flaked almond on top of each macaroon; bake in very slow oven about 1 hour or until firm and dry. Cool on trays.

Makes about 25.
- Recipe can be made a week ahead.
- Storage: Airtight container.
- Freeze: Suitable.
- Microwave: Not suitable.

Macaroons, Coconut

Although almonds were the key ingredient in traditional macaroons, coconut quickly became an equally popular adaptation.

2 egg whites
½ cup caster sugar
1 teaspoon vanilla essence
2 tablespoons plain flour
1½ cups (140g) coconut
6 glace cherries, quartered

Beat egg whites in small bowl with electric mixer until soft peaks form. Gradually add sugar, beating until dissolved between additions. Stir in essence, sifted flour and coconut in 2 batches.

Line oven trays with baking paper. Drop level tablespoons of mixture into trays about 5cm apart. Place a cherry quarter on top of each macaroon; bake in slow oven about 40 minutes or until lightly browned, cool on trays.

Makes about 25.
- Recipe can be made a week ahead.
- Storage: Airtight container.
- Freeze: Suitable.
- Microwave: Not suitable.

Madeira Cake

This cake does not actually contain madeira. It is a plain cake, always topped with peel, and was served with a glass of madeira in Victorian England.

180g butter, softened
2 teaspoons grated lemon rind
⅔ cup caster sugar
3 eggs
¾ cup plain flour
¾ cup self-raising flour
⅓ cup mixed peel
¼ cup slivered almonds

Grease deep 20cm round cake pan; line base with paper, grease paper.

Beat butter, rind and sugar in small bowl with electric mixer until light and fluffy; beat in eggs 1 at a time, beat until combined. Transfer mixture to large bowl, stir in sifted flours. Spread mixture into prepared pan, bake in moderately slow oven 20 minutes. Sprinkle peel and nuts evenly over cake. Bake about further 40 minutes. Stand cake 5 minutes before turning onto wire rack to cool.

■ Cake can be made a day ahead.
■ Storage: Airtight container.
■ Freeze: Suitable.
■ Microwave: Not suitable.

Marble Cake

We've chosen the traditional children's party favourite combination of pink, white and chocolate, but there are many other equally attractive possibilities. Vary the colours and essence to suit your own preferences.

180g butter
1 teaspoon vanilla essence
¾ cup caster sugar
2 eggs
1½ cups self-raising flour
½ cup milk
pink food colouring
2 tablespoons cocoa
1 tablespoon milk, extra

ICING

90g butter
1 cup icing sugar
1½ tablespoons milk
pink food colouring

Lightly grease 20cm ring cake pan, cover base with paper, grease paper.

Beat butter, essence and caster sugar in small bowl with electric mixer until mixture is light and fluffy. Add eggs 1 at a time, beating well between additions. Transfer mixture to large bowl, fold in sifted flour and milk in 2 batches. Divide mixture evenly between 3 bowls.

Tint mixture pink in 1 bowl; mix well. Stir sifted cocoa and extra milk into another bowl; mix well. Drop spoonfuls of each mixture into prepared pan. Run a knife through cake mixture for a marbled effect. Bake in moderate oven about 40 minutes. Stand cake 5 minutes before turning onto wire rack to cool.

Drop alternate spoonfuls of pink and white icing on top of cold cake. Using a spatula swirl icing to give marbled effect.

Icing: Beat butter in small bowl with electric mixer until as white as possible, beat in sifted icing sugar and milk in 2 batches. Divide mixture between 2 bowls, use colouring to tint mixture pink in 1 bowl.

- Cake can be made a day ahead.
- Storage: Airtight container.
- Freeze: Suitable
- Microwave: Not suitable.

BELOW LEFT: Madeira Cake.
BELOW: Marble Cake.

Below left: Plate from Royal Doulton; tablecloth from Aginian's. Below: China from Mikasa; tablecloth from Belinda's Corner.

Marshmallow Pavlova

While meringue cake (known as vacherin in France and Spanish Wind Cake in Austria) has been known for almost two centuries, the Pavlova, with its marshmallow-like inside, is said to have been the invention of Perth chef Bert Sachse in the 1930s. It was so named by his employers because it was considered to be as light as the dancer, Anna Pavlova. However, there is also a claim by New Zealanders that it was their creation, and indeed a similar cake was known there at about the same time.

4 egg whites
1 cup caster sugar
1 tablespoon cornflour
1 teaspoon white vinegar
300ml carton thickened cream
2 teaspoons vanilla essence
1 tablespoon icing sugar

Cover oven tray with baking paper, mark 18cm circle in paper.

Beat egg whites in small bowl with electric mixer until soft peaks form; gradually add caster sugar, beat until dissolved between additions. Fold in cornflour and vinegar. Spread meringue inside circle on prepared tray. For best results do not squash or flatten mixture but shape side up and in toward the centre, like a mound. Make furrows up side of pavlova using small spatula, level top.

Bake in very slow oven about 1¼ hours or until dry. Turn oven off, leave to cool in oven with door ajar.

An hour before serving, beat cream, essence and sifted icing sugar until soft peaks form. Fill pavlova with cream mixture, decorate with fruit of your choice.
Serves 6 to 8.
■ Pavlova can be made 4 days ahead.
■ Storage: Airtight container.
■ Freeze: Not suitable.
■ Microwave: Not suitable.

Matches

2 sheets ready-rolled puff pastry
⅔ cup strawberry jam
300ml carton thickened cream

LEMON ICING
1 cup icing sugar
1 teaspoon lemon juice
1 tablespoon milk, approximately

CHOCOLATE ICING
¼ cup icing sugar
1 tablespoon cocoa
3 teaspoons milk, approximately

Bake pastry sheets on ungreased oven trays in moderately hot oven about 10 minutes, or until sheets are lightly browned and puffed. Turn onto wire rack, cool, smooth sides up.

Spread jam over smooth side of 1 sheet of pastry. Beat cream in small bowl until soft peaks form; spread over jam, top with remaining pastry; press pastry gently. Working quickly, spread pastry with lemon icing, place chocolate icing in piping bag fitted with small plain tube. Pipe chocolate at 2cm intervals over lemon icing. For a feather effect run skewer in opposite direction across lines of icing at 2cm intervals. Cut into rectangles with serrated or electric knife when set.

Lemon Icing: Sift icing sugar into small bowl, stir in juice and enough milk to make spreadable.

Chocolate Icing: Sift icing sugar and cocoa into small bowl; stir in enough milk to make spreadable.
Makes 8.
■ Recipe can be made a day ahead.
■ Storage: Covered, in refrigerator.
■ Freeze: Not suitable.
■ Microwave: Not suitable.

LEFT: Marshmallow Pavlova.
RIGHT: Matches.

Left: Plate from Waterford Wedgwood; tablecloth from Belinda's Corner. Right: Plate from Villeroy & Boch; lace cloth and wooden tray from Belinda's Corner.

Melting Moments

Also known as yo yos, these delectable treats have a long history – a recipe for them is included in the Australian section of Mrs Beeton's 'Cookery and Household Management'.

125g butter
1 teaspoon vanilla essence
2 tablespoons icing sugar
¾ cup plain flour
¼ cup cornflour
FILLING
30g butter
½ teaspoon vanilla essence
½ cup icing sugar
1 teaspoon milk, approximately

Beat butter, essence and sifted icing sugar in small bowl with electric mixer until light and fluffy. Stir in sifted flours. Spoon mixture into piping bag fitted with a 1cm fluted tube. Pipe 3cm rosettes about 3cm apart onto lightly greased oven trays. Bake in moderate oven about 10 minutes or until lightly browned; cool on trays. Join cold biscuits with filling.

Filling: Beat butter, essence and sifted icing sugar in small bowl until light and fluffy; beat in enough milk to make mixture spreadable.

Makes about 20.

- Recipe can be made 2 days ahead.
- Storage: Airtight container.
- Freeze: Unfilled biscuits suitable.
- Microwave: Not suitable.

Monte Carlos

Monte Carlo, the famous Monaco gambling resort, was very much associated with glamour, high living and the rich and famous in the years before and after World War II. Monte Carlo's fame was the inspiration for a delicious and rather extravagant new commercial line invented by Arnott's Biscuits, around the 1930s.

180g butter
1 teaspoon vanilla essence
½ cup brown sugar, firmly packed
1 egg
1¼ cups self-raising flour
¾ cup plain flour
¼ teaspoon bicarbonate of soda
⅔ cup coconut
⅓ cup raspberry jam, approximately

VIENNA CREAM

60g butter
½ teaspoon vanilla essence
¾ cup icing sugar
2 teaspoons milk

Beat butter, essence and sugar in small bowl with electric mixer until just combined, add egg, beat only until combined. Stir in sifted flours, soda and coconut in 2 batches. Roll 2 level teaspoons of mixture into ovals, place onto greased oven trays about 5cm apart, flatten slightly; use back of fork to roughen surface. Bake in moderately hot oven about 7 minutes. Lift biscuits onto wire rack to cool. Sandwich biscuits with Vienna cream and jam.

Vienna Cream: Beat butter, essence and sifted icing sugar in small bowl with electric mixer until fluffy, beat in milk.

Makes about 28.
- Recipe can be made a week ahead.
- Storage: Airtight container.
- Freeze: Unfilled biscuits suitable.
- Microwave: Not suitable.

Mushrooms

It is important to have the milk and butter at room temperature when making the butter cream filling.

90g butter
1 teaspoon vanilla essence
⅓ cup caster sugar
1 egg
1⅔ cups plain flour
⅓ cup raspberry jam, approximately
⅓ cup crushed mixed nuts, approximately
2 teaspoons cocoa, approximately

FILLING

90g butter
½ teaspoon vanilla essence
⅓ cup caster sugar
⅓ cup milk
⅓ cup water

Grease 2½ 12 hole shallow patty pans.

Beat butter, essence and sugar in small bowl with electric mixer until smooth and creamy. Add egg, beat until just combined; stir in sifted flour. Turn mixture onto lightly floured surface, knead gently until smooth; cover, refrigerate 30 minutes.

Roll pastry on lightly floured surface until 2mm thick, cut 6½cm rounds from pastry, place in prepared trays. To make stalks, roll pastry scaps to 8mm diameter sausage, cut 30 stalks 1½cm long; place on lightly greased oven tray. Bake cases and stalks in moderately hot oven about 12 minutes or until lightly browned. Flatten pastry cases with back of spoon halfway through cooking to remove air bubbles. Cool on wire racks.

Spread inside of each pastry case with about ½ teaspoon jam, sprinkle with about ½ teaspoon nuts. Spread about 2 level teaspoons filling into each case, sprinkle with a little sifted cocoa. Press stalks into filling.

Filling: Have butter and milk at room temperature. Beat butter, essence and sugar in small bowl with electric mixer until as white as possible. Gradually beat in milk and water a teaspoon at a time.

Makes about 30.
- Pastry cases can be prepared 2 days ahead.
- Storage: Airtight container.
- Freeze: Pastry cases suitable.
- Microwave: Not suitable.

FAR LEFT: Melting Moments.
LEFT: Monte Carlos.
ABOVE: Mushrooms.

Far left: Tablecloth from Belinda's Corner; crystal vase from Royal Doulton.

79

Napoleon Cake

The exact origin of this cake is unknown, although it is almost certainly an adaptation of the French Napolitains. These were elaborate cakes, consisting of layers of pastry and fruit puree, which formed the centrepiece of grand buffet tables. The American version of Napoleons includes cream and jam while in Australia and New Zealand, sponge cake is used for the middle layer. A very old British version is called Westmorland Three-Tier Cake.

2 sheets ready-rolled puff pastry
½ cup raspberry jam

SPONGE
2 eggs
1 teaspoon vanilla essence
⅓ cup caster sugar
⅓ cup self-raising flour
2 tablespoons cornflour

MOCK CREAM
½ cup sugar
⅓ cup water
125g unsalted butter

PASSIONFRUIT ICING
1 cup icing sugar
1 teaspoon soft butter
1 passionfruit
1 teaspoon milk, approximately

Bake pastry sheets on ungreased oven trays in moderately hot oven about 10 minutes or until lightly browned and puffed. Gently flatten puffed parts of pastry with back of spoon; cool pastry.

Assemble cake by spreading 1 pastry sheet with half the cream; spread 1 side of sponge with half the jam, place on cream. Spread sponge with remaining jam and cream. Top with remaining pastry sheet, spread with passionfruit icing. When set, cut with serrated or electric knife.

Sponge: Grease 23cm square slab pan. Beat eggs and essence in small bowl with electric mixer until thick; gradually add sugar, beat until dissolved between additions. Triple sift flours, fold into egg mixture, spread into prepared pan. Bake in moderate oven about 15 minutes. Turn immediately onto wire rack to cool.

Mock Cream: Combine sugar and water in small pan, stir over heat without boiling until sugar is dissolved; remove from heat, cool. Beat butter in small bowl with electric mixer until as white as possible; gradually beat in cold syrup.

Passionfruit Icing: Sift icing sugar into small heatproof bowl, stir in butter, passionfruit pulp and enough milk to mix to a stiff paste. Stir icing over hot water until spreadable.

■ Recipe can be made a day ahead.
■ Storage: Covered, in refrigerator.
■ Freeze: Not suitable.
■ Microwave: Not suitable.

Neenish Tarts

1½ cups plain flour
100g butter
1 egg yolk
2 tablespoons lemon juice, approximately

MOCK CREAM
1½ tablespoons milk
¾ cup sugar
¼ cup water
½ teaspoon gelatine
1½ tablespoons water, extra
180g unsalted butter
1 teaspoon vanilla essence

GLACE ICING
1½ cups icing sugar
2 tablespoons milk
½ teaspoon vanilla essence
1½ tablespoons cocoa
1½ teaspoons milk, extra

Grease 2 x 12-hole shallow patty pans.

Sift flour into bowl, rub in butter. Stir in yolk and enough juice to make ingredients cling together. Press dough into ball, knead gently on lightly floured surface until smooth; cover, refrigerate dough 30 minutes.

Roll pastry on lightly floured surface to 3mm thick, cut into 7cm rounds, place into prepared pans, prick pastry all over with fork. Bake in moderate oven about 12 minutes or until golden brown. Lift onto wire racks to cool.

Fill pastry cases with mock cream, level tops with spatula. Spread a teaspoon of vanilla icing over half of each tart, allow to set. Cover remaining half of each tart with chocolate icing.

Mock Cream: Combine milk, sugar and water in pan, stir over heat, without boiling, until sugar is dissolved. Sprinkle gelatine over extra water, stir into milk mixture, stir until dissolved; cool.

Beat butter and essence in small bowl with electric mixer until as white as possible, gradually add cold milk mixture; beat until light and fluffy. Mixture will thicken on standing.

Glace Icing: Sift icing sugar into small bowl, stir in milk and essence, beat until smooth; divide into 2 heatproof bowls. Stir sifted cocoa and extra milk into 1 bowl. Stir both icings over hot water until icing is smooth and spreadable.

Makes 24.

■ Recipe can be made 2 days ahead.
■ Storage: Covered, in refrigerator.
■ Freeze: Not suitable.
■ Microwave: Not suitable.

Nesselrode Ice-Cream

This iced pudding was invented in the 17th century by a Monsieur Mouy, who was the French chef of the Russian statesman Count Nesselrode. It was once extremely popular and in some places is now served as traditional Christmas fare.

This ice-cream can also be frozen in an 8 cup capacity steamer or mould.

⅓ cup finely chopped glace apricots
2 tablespoons brandy
300ml carton thickened cream
4 eggs, separated
½ cup icing sugar
250g can sweetened chestnut spread
toasted flaked almonds

APRICOT SAUCE
1 cup (150g) finely chopped dried apricots
1 cup water
1¼ cups orange juice

Combine apricots and brandy in small bowl; stand 20 minutes. Whip cream until soft peaks form.

Beat egg whites in small bowl with electric mixer until soft peaks form. Add sifted sugar gradually, beat until dissolved. Transfer mixture to large bowl; fold in cream, egg yolks, apricot mixture and chestnut spread. Pour mixture into loaf pan, cover, freeze overnight. Serve with apricot sauce and flaked almonds.

Apricot Sauce: Combine apricots and water in pan, bring to boil; simmer, covered, about 10 minutes or until pulpy; cool. Blend or process apricot mixture and juice until smooth; strain.

Serves 8.

■ Recipe can be made 3 days ahead.
■ Storage: Ice-cream, covered, in freezer. Sauce, covered, in refrigerator.
■ Microwave: Sauce suitable.

FAR LEFT: Napoleon Cake.
ABOVE LEFT: Neenish Tarts.
LEFT: Nesselrode Ice-Cream.

Old English Matrimonials

There are numerous versions of this very old English recipe and almost as many names. The connection with matrimony is thought to have come about because of the slightly rough appearance of the cakes (a result of the oats, an important ingredient in this recipe), just as in the state of marriage, the consumer must take the rough with the smooth!

1½ cups self-raising flour
180g butter
1 cup brown sugar, firmly packed
1 cup (90g) coconut
⅓ cup rolled oats
¾ cup raspberry jam

Grease 20cm x 30cm lamington pan. Sift flour into large bowl, rub in butter. Stir in sugar, coconut and oats. Press half the mixture firmly over base of prepared pan, spread with jam. Sprinkle remaining mixture over jam, press down lightly. Bake in moderate oven about 30 minutes or until browned. Cool in pan before cutting.

■ Recipe can be made 2 days ahead.
■ Storage: Airtight container.
■ Freeze: Suitable.
■ Microwave: Not suitable.

BELOW: From left: Orange Cake, Old English Matrimonials.
BELOW RIGHT: Palmiers.

Below: Cake tin from The Cottage Manner.

Orange Cake

It is almost impossible to imagine life without the versatile, everyday orange, but when oranges were first introduced to the West more than 400 years ago, they were treated as ornamental plants only. Native to South-East Asia, they were first cultivated in India and in fact our name for them is derived from the Sanskrit word naranja.

150g butter
1 tablespoon grated orange rind
⅔ cup caster sugar
3 eggs
1½ cups self-raising flour
¼ cup milk

ORANGE ICING

1½ cups icing sugar
1 teaspoon soft butter
1 tablespoon orange juice,
approximately

Grease deep 20cm round cake pan.

Combine all ingredients in medium bowl, beat with electric mixer at low speed until just combined. Increase speed to medium, beat about 3 minutes or until mixture is smooth. Spread mixture into prepared pan; bake in moderate oven about 40 minutes. Stand cake 5 minutes before turning onto wire rack to cool. Spread cold cake with orange icing.

Orange Icing: Sift icing sugar into small heatproof bowl, stir in butter and enough juice to form a stiff paste. Stir icing over hot water until spreadable.

■ Recipe can be made 2 days ahead.
■ Storage: Airtight container.
■ Freeze: Suitable.
■ Microwave: Not suitable.

Palmiers

These small pastries are an old Paris speciality, probably invented as a clever way to use up scraps of puff pastry. They are quick and easy to make for an afternoon tea.

375g packet frozen puff pastry,
thawed
2 tablespoons caster sugar,
approximately

Roll pastry on surface sprinkled with sugar to 20cm x 35cm rectangle; trim edges with sharp knife. Sprinkle pastry lightly with a little more sugar. Fold in long sides of rectangle so they meet in the centre, sprinkle with a little more sugar, fold in half lengthways, press lightly; cover, refrigerate 30 minutes.

Cut pastry roll into 12mm slices, place about 10cm apart onto lightly greased oven trays, bake in moderately hot oven 10 minutes, turn palmiers with egg slide, bake about further 10 minutes or until crisp. Lift onto wire racks to cool. Lightly dust with sifted icing sugar, if desired.

Makes about 25.

■ Recipe can be made 2 days ahead.
■ Storage: Airtight container.
■ Freeze: Uncooked suitable.
■ Microwave: Not suitable.

Pancakes

It is thought by many food historians that pancakes were probably the first 'recipe' ever invented by primitive cooks, in the form of grain meal and water, cooked on hot stones. Almost every culture's cuisine has a version, from France's crepes to Mexico's tortillas. In Britain, it became customary to eat pancakes on Shrove Tuesday, as a way to use up milk, butter and eggs which were forbidden during Lent. Even today, Pancake Tuesday is celebrated, although without any religious significance for many people.

2 cups plain flour
4 eggs, lightly beaten
2 cups milk
butter
¼ cup lemon juice, approximately
2 tablespoons sugar,
    approximately

Sift flour into bowl, gradually add combined eggs and milk; mix, or blend or process, until mixture is smooth. Cover, stand 30 minutes.

Lightly grease heated heavy-based pan with butter, pour about ¼ cup batter evenly into pan. Cook pancake until lightly browned underneath; turn, cook until lightly browned on other side. Keep pancakes warm while cooking remaining batter. Serve pancakes sprinkled with lemon juice and sugar. Makes about 15.

■ Recipe best made close to serving.
■ Freeze: Suitable.
■ Microwave: Not suitable.

Passionfruit Flummery

Flummery, or Frumenty as it was sometimes called, seems to have originated in rural Britain where it was made with oatmeal or wheat ears soaked in warm water for up to 3 days, and eaten as a variation on breakfast porridge. Over time, the grain disappeared from the recipe and fruit and gelatine (or isinglass, before gelatine was invented) were added, turning it into a jelly-like dessert. The word comes from the Welsh Ilymru and also means 'agreeable humbug'.

BELOW: Pancakes.
RIGHT: From back: Passionfruit Flummery, Peach Melba.

Right: China from Mikasa.

3 teaspoons gelatine
½ cup caster sugar
2 tablespoons plain flour
¾ cup water
1 cup fresh orange juice, strained
⅔ cup passionfruit pulp

Combine gelatine, sugar and flour in pan, gradually stir in water. Stir over heat until mixture boils and thickens; transfer to medium bowl, stir in juice and passionfruit pulp. Refrigerate until mixture starts to set around edge of bowl.

Beat mixture with electric mixer for about 10 minutes or until thick and creamy. Pour into 6 serving glasses (¾ cup capacity), cover, refrigerate until set. Serve with cream and extra passionfruit pulp, if desired.
Serves 6.
■ Recipe can be made a day ahead.
■ Storage: Covered, in refrigerator.
■ Freeze: Not suitable.
■ Microwave: Suitable.

Peach Melba

This splendid dessert was created in 1892 by Escoffier, chef at London's Savoy Hotel, in honour of Dame Nellie Melba, after a concert at the hotel.

If fresh peaches are not available, canned peaches can be substituted. If desired, berries can be blended or processed instead of strained, but often the tiny seeds, when pulverised, can give a bitter taste to the sauce.

2 cups water
4 fresh firm peaches
vanilla ice-cream

RASPBERRY SAUCE
200g fresh or frozen raspberries
1 tablespoon icing sugar,
approximately

Place water in pan, bring to boil, add peaches, simmer 5 minutes. Remove peaches from water, place in bowl of cold water. When peaches are cold, remove skins; cut peaches in half, remove stones. Serve peach halves topped with ice-cream and raspberry sauce.

Raspberry Sauce: Push raspberries through fine strainer, sweeten pulp with sifted icing sugar to taste.
Serves 4.
■ Recipe best made close to serving.
■ Freeze: Not suitable.
■ Microwave: Not suitable.

Peanut Slice

60g butter
2 tablespoons caster sugar
1 egg, lightly beaten
1 cup plain flour
2 tablespoons self-raising flour
¼ cup raspberry jam

TOPPING

2 eggs, separated
¾ cup caster sugar
30g butter, melted
1 cup (90g) coconut
1½ cups (250g) chopped roasted
    unsalted peanuts
1 cup (30g) Corn Flakes

Grease 20cm x 30cm lamington pan.
Beat butter and sugar in small bowl with electric mixer until creamy; gradually add egg, beat until combined. Stir in sifted flours. Press mixture over base of prepared pan, prick well with fork. Bake in moderately hot oven about 10 minutes or until base is firm; cool.

Spread jam over base, spread topping over jam. Bake in moderate oven about 30 minutes or until browned and firm; cool in pan. Refrigerate 1 hour before cutting.

Topping: Beat egg yolks, sugar and butter in small bowl until thick and creamy, stir in coconut and peanuts. Beat egg whites in small bowl until soft peaks form, fold into nut mixture with Corn Flakes.

■ Recipe can be made 3 days ahead.
■ Storage: Airtight container.
■ Freeze: Suitable.
■ Microwave: Not suitable.

Pecan Pie

The pecan, which grows in a limited area in Mexico and the southern United States, was largely introduced to the rest of the world through America's famous pecan pie.

1 cup plain flour
90g butter
2 tablespoons water, approximately

FILLING

3 eggs, lightly beaten
¾ cup light corn syrup or glucose
    syrup
1 cup brown sugar, firmly packed
30g butter, melted
1¼ cups (125g) pecan nuts

Sift flour into bowl, rub in butter. Add enough water to make ingredients cling together. Press dough into ball, knead gently on lightly floured surface until smooth; cover, refrigerate 30 minutes.

Roll dough on lightly floured surface large enough to line 24cm round loose-based flan tin. Lift pastry into tin gently, ease into side, trim edge. Place tin on oven tray, line pastry with paper, fill with dried beans or rice. Bake in moderately hot oven 10 minutes, remove paper and beans, bake further 10 minutes or until pastry is lightly browned; cool.

Pour filling into pastry case, bake in moderately slow oven 55 minutes or until set; cool.

Filling: Combine eggs, corn syrup, sugar, butter and nuts in bowl; mix well.

Serves 6 to 8.
■ Recipe can be made 2 days ahead.
■ Storage: Airtight container.
■ Freeze: Suitable.
■ Microwave: Suitable.

*LEFT: From top: Pecan Pie, Peanut Slice.
BELOW: Pikelets.*

Left: China from Mikasa.

Pikelets

Pikelets are the Midlands, North England and Scottish version of the southern British crumpet. During cold British winters, they are indispensable afternoon tea items.

Use electric frypan, frying pan or solid plate over griller for cooking pikelets. Turn pikelets just before the bubbles burst for best results.

1 cup self-raising flour
¼ cup caster sugar
pinch bicarbonate of soda
1 egg, lightly beaten
¾ cup milk, approximately

Sift dry ingredients into medium bowl. Make well in centre, gradually stir in egg and enough milk to give a smooth, creamy, pouring consistency.

Drop dessertspoons of batter from tip of spoon into heated greased frying pan; allow room for spreading. When bubbles begin to appear, turn pikelets, cook until lightly browned on other side. Serve warm with butter or cream and jam.

Makes about 15.
■ Recipe best made just before serving.
■ Freeze: Suitable.
■ Microwave: Not suitable.

Plum Pudding With Hard Sauce

This stunning but plum-less Christmas Pudding wasn't so-named in a fit of typical British humour, as some may think; its earliest ancestor was a kind of plum porridge. Early in the 18th century, the pudding became less and less liquid, developing into the splendid solid mass of spiced fruit that is now traditionally served at the end of Christmas dinner. The name remains, although the plums have long disappeared from the recipe. Also gone, at least in Australia, is the custom of cooking good-luck coins in the pudding, because the metal used to mint decimal currency coins, introduced in 1966, is not suitable.

You will need a 60cm square of unbleached calico for this recipe.

1½ cups (250g) raisins, chopped
1½ cups (250g) sultanas
1¼ cups (190g) currants
1 cup (170g) mixed peel
1 teaspoon grated lemon rind
2 tablespoons lemon juice

2 tablespoons brandy
250g butter
2 cups (400g) brown sugar, firmly packed
5 eggs
1¼ cups plain flour
½ teaspoon ground nutmeg
½ teaspoon mixed spice

4 cups (280g) stale breadcrumbs, lightly packed
½ cup plain flour, extra

HARD SAUCE
125g unsalted butter
2 cups icing sugar
1 tablespoon brandy

Soak a 60cm square of unbleached calico in cold water overnight. Next day, boil in water 20 minutes, rinse well.

Combine fruit, rind, juice and brandy in large bowl, mix well; cover, stand overnight or up to a week.

Beat butter and sugar in large bowl with electric mixer only until combined. Beat in eggs 1 at a time, beat only until combined between additions. Add creamed mixture to fruit mixture, add sifted flour, nutmeg, spice and breadcrumbs in 2 batches; mix well.

Dip prepared calico into boiling water, wring excess water from cloth. Spread hot cloth onto bench, quickly rub extra flour into centre of cloth to cover an area about 40cm in diameter, leaving flour thicker in the centre.

Place pudding mixture in centre of cloth, gather edges of cloth together, pat into round shape. Tie cloth securely and tightly with string, close to pudding mixture. There is no need to leave room for the pudding to expand during the cooking process.

Lower pudding into large pan or boiler of boiling water. Pudding must have plenty of water to move in. It will sink to the bottom of the pan at first, but will float to the top after about 20 to 30 minutes. Boil, covered, 6 hours, replenishing the boiling water as it evaporates. Lift pudding from water. Suspend about 10 minutes or until cloth looks dry. Turn pudding out of cloth, cool to room temperature.

Wrap pudding in clean, dry cloth, secure with string again, place in plastic bag, refrigerate.

Reheat pudding by boiling for 2 hours on day of serving. Remove cloth from pudding, stand 10 to 20 minutes before serving. Serve with hard sauce.

Hard Sauce: Beat butter in small bowl with electric mixer until light and fluffy, gradually beat in sifted icing sugar and brandy. Refrigerate until firm.

Serves 8 to 10.

- Pudding can be made 3 months ahead. Butter can be made a week ahead.
- Storage: Pudding, in airtight bag, in refrigerator. Sauce, covered, in refrigerator.
- Freeze: Pudding and sauce suitable.
- Microwave: Reheating single serves of pudding suitable.

LEFT: Plum Pudding with Hard Sauce.
ABOVE: Pound Cake.

Left: China from Mikasa.

Pound Cake

This cake takes its name from the fact that originally, and certainly pre-metric conversion, it was made with a pound each of butter, sugar and flour. Somehow '250g Cake' just doesn't have the same ring to it!

250g butter
1 teaspoon vanilla essence
1 cup caster sugar
4 eggs
½ cup self-raising flour
1 cup plain flour

Grease deep 20cm round cake pan; line base with paper; grease paper.

Beat butter, essence and sugar in small bowl with electric mixer until light and fluffy. Add eggs 1 at a time, beating well between additions. Transfer mixture to large bowl, fold in sifted flours in 2 batches. Spread mixture into prepared pan, bake in moderate oven about 1 hour. Stand cake 5 minutes before turning onto wire rack to cool.

- Cake can be made 3 days ahead.
- Storage: Airtight container.
- Freeze: Suitable.
- Microwave: Not suitable.

Pumpkin Scones

Whatever the outcome of her political career, Flo Bjelke-Petersen will long be remembered in Australia for her championing of the pumpkin scone.

You will need to cook about 250g pumpkin for this recipe.

40g butter
¼ cup caster sugar
1 egg, lightly beaten
¾ cup cooked mashed pumpkin
2½ cups self-raising flour
½ teaspoon ground nutmeg
⅓ cup milk, approximately

Pumpkin Pie

In Central Europe, pumpkin is largely considered to be animal fodder rather than food for humans, while in France it is used to make soups, jams and desserts. Perhaps the most well-known pumpkin recipe comes to us, from America, in the form of this delicious pie.

You will need to cook about 350g pumpkin for this recipe.

1 cup plain flour
¼ cup self-raising flour
2 tablespoons cornflour
2 tablespoons icing sugar
125g butter, chopped
2 tablespoons water,
   approximately

FILLING
2 eggs
¼ cup brown sugar
2 tablespoons maple syrup
1 cup cooked mashed pumpkin
⅔ cup evaporated milk
1 teaspoon ground cinnamon
½ teaspoon ground nutmeg
pinch ground allspice

Sift flours and sugar into bowl, rub in butter. Add enough water to make ingredients cling together. Press dough into a ball, knead gently on floured surface until smooth; cover, refrigerate 30 minutes.

Roll pastry on lightly floured surface large enough to line 23cm pie plate, make a double edge of pastry, trim and decorate edge. Cover pastry with paper, fill with dried beans or rice. Bake in moderately hot oven 10 minutes. Remove paper and beans, bake about further 10 minutes or until lightly browned; cool.

Pour filling into pastry case, bake in moderate oven about 50 minutes or until filling is set; cool. Lightly dust with extra sifted icing sugar, if desired.

Filling: Beat eggs, sugar and maple syrup in small bowl with electric mixer until thick. Stir in pumpkin, milk and spices.

Serves 6 to 8.
■ Recipe can be made a day ahead.
■ Storage: Covered, in refrigerator.
■ Freeze: Not suitable.
■ Microwave: Not suitable.

ABOVE: Pumpkin Pie.
ABOVE RIGHT: Queen of Puddings.
RIGHT: Pumpkin Scones.

Lightly grease 2 x 20cm round sandwich pans. Beat butter and sugar in small bowl with electric mixer until light and fluffy, gradually beat in egg; transfer to large bowl. Stir in pumpkin, then sifted dry ingredients and enough milk to make a soft sticky dough. Turn dough onto lightly floured surface, knead lightly until smooth. Press dough out to about 2cm in thickness, cut 5cm rounds from dough. Place scones, just touching, in prepared pans. Brush tops with a little milk. Bake in very hot oven about 15 minutes. Makes about 16.

■ Recipe best made just before serving.
■ Freeze: Suitable.
■ Microwave: Not suitable.

Queen of Puddings

Also called Queen Pudding, this dish, based on a 17th century version, was created for Queen Victoria by her chefs at Buckingham Palace.

Pink sugar gives a pretty finish to this dessert. The easy clean way to colour sugar is to put the sugar in a plastic bag with a tiny drop of colouring, then rub the colouring through the sugar by rubbing and kneading through the plastic bag. Any excess sugar will keep indefinitely in a jar.

2 cups (140g) stale breadcrumbs
1 tablespoon caster sugar
2 teaspoons vanilla essence
1 teaspoon grated lemon rind
2½ cups milk
60g butter
4 eggs, separated
¼ cup raspberry jam
¾ cup caster sugar, extra
2 teaspoons crystal sugar
pink food colouring

Combine breadcrumbs, caster sugar, essence and rind in large bowl. Heat milk and butter in pan until almost boiling, stir into bread mixture; stand 10 minutes.

Stir yolks into bread mixture, pour into shallow ovenproof dish (5 cup capacity). Bake, uncovered, in moderate oven about 35 minutes or until set.

Carefully spread top of pudding with warmed jam. Beat egg whites in small bowl with electric mixer until soft peaks form, gradually add extra caster sugar, beat until sugar is dissolved. Spread meringue over pudding, bake in moderate oven about 10 minutes or until lightly coloured. Tint crystal sugar pink, sprinkle over hot pudding.
Serves 6 to 8.

■ Recipe best made just before serving.
■ Freeze: Not suitable.
■ Microwave: Not suitable.

Rainbow Cake

4 eggs
1½ cups caster sugar
2 cups self-raising flour
1 cup hot milk
50g butter, melted
2 tablespoons cocoa
2 tablespoons milk, extra
pink food colouring
1 teaspoon vanilla essence
¾ cup thickened cream
FLUFFY FROSTING
1 cup sugar
½ cup water
2 egg whites
food colouring

Grease 3 x 20cm round sandwich pans, line bases with paper, grease paper.

Beat eggs in medium bowl with electric mixer until thick and creamy; gradually add sugar, beat until dissolved between additions. Transfer mixture to large bowl, fold in sifted flour and combined hot milk and butter in 2 batches. Divide mixture evenly into 3 bowls. Blend sifted cocoa with extra milk, fold into 1 portion. Tint another portion pink with colouring and stir essence into remaining portion.

Pour mixtures into prepared pans. Bake in moderate oven about 25 minutes, alternate position of pans in oven after 15 minutes. Turn cakes immediately onto wire racks to cool.

Beat cream until firm peaks form. Place chocolate cake onto serving plate, spread with half the cream, top with pink cake, spread with remaining cream, top with vanilla cake. Spread frosting all over cake, decorate as desired.

Fluffy Frosting: Combine sugar and water in pan, stir over heat, without boiling, until sugar is dissolved. Boil, without stirring, until sugar syrup is thick but not coloured (114°C on candy thermometer).

Beat egg whites in small bowl with electric mixer until soft peaks form; with motor operating, gradually beat in hot sugar syrup in a thin stream. Tint with colouring, if desired. Continue beating until thick and cool.

- Recipe can be made a day ahead.
- Storage: Covered, in refrigerator.
- Freeze: Unfilled, unfrosted cakes suitable.
- Microwave: Not suitable.

Rice Custard

Use leftover rice or boil about 2 tablespoons of rice for this recipe.

3 eggs
⅓ cup caster sugar
1 teaspoon vanilla essence
2½ cups milk
½ cup cooked rice
¼ cup sultanas
ground cinnamon or ground nutmeg

Whisk eggs, sugar, essence and milk together in medium bowl; stir in rice and sultanas. Pour mixture into 4 ovenproof dishes (1 cup capacity). Place dishes into baking dish, add enough boiling water to come halfway up sides of dishes. Bake in moderate oven 35 minutes.

Sprinkle custard lightly with cinnamon, bake further 15 minutes or until just set. Serve warm or cold with cream, if desired.
Serves 4.

- Recipe can be made 3 days ahead.
- Storage: Covered, in refrigerator.
- Freeze: Not suitable.
- Microwave: Not suitable.

Rice Pudding

This creamy pudding is perhaps the most loved and homely of British desserts.

½ cup short-grain rice
2½ cups milk
¼ cup caster sugar
2 tablespoons sultanas
1 teaspoon vanilla essence
2 teaspoons butter
ground nutmeg or ground cinnamon

Lightly grease shallow ovenproof dish (4 cup capacity).

Wash rice well under cold water; drain well. Combine rice, milk, sugar, sultanas, and essence in prepared dish, mix lightly with a fork. Dot top with butter, sprinkle lightly with nutmeg. Bake in moderately slow oven about 2 hours or until most of the milk has been absorbed. Serve warm or cold with fruit, if desired.
Serves 4.

- Recipe can be made a day ahead.
- Storage: Covered, in refrigerator.
- Freeze: Not suitable.
- Microwave: Not suitable.

RIGHT: From front: Rice Custard, Rice Pudding.
LEFT: Rainbow Cake.

Right: Tiles from The Olde English Tile Factory.

Rich Fruit Cake

This splendid cake has been the centrepiece of wedding, Christmas, christening and other special occasion tables for several decades – not surprising, as it looks wonderful, tasted delicious and keeps extremely well.

The cake can be covered in almond or marzipan paste; you will need 500g paste to cover a 23cm round cake. Knead the paste with a little sifted pure icing sugar until the paste loses its stickiness. Brush the cake liberally but evenly with lightly beaten egg white. Roll the paste out on a surface lightly dusted with sifted icing sugar, large enough to cover the cake. Lift the paste onto the cake with rolling pin, smooth out folds with sugared hands. Trim excess paste away. Leave cake to stand for a day. Use a 2 egg white quantity of fluffy frosting (see page 92) to cover the cake, or buy 750g packaged soft icing and roll it out large enough to cover the almond pasted cake.

3 cups (500g) sultanas
1½ cups (250g) raisins, chopped
¾ cup currants
½ cup mixed peel
⅔ cup glace cherries, quartered
2 tablespoons marmalade
½ cup dark rum or brandy
250g butter
1 teaspoon grated orange rind
1 teaspoon grated lemon rind
1 cup brown sugar, firmly packed
4 eggs
2 cups plain flour
2 teaspoons mixed spice
2 tablespoons dark rum or brandy, extra

Line deep 23cm round or deep 19cm square cake pan with 3 layers of baking paper. Bring paper 5cm above edge of pan.

Combine fruit, marmalade and rum in large bowl; mix well, stand overnight.

Beat butter and rinds in small bowl with electric mixer until just smooth; add sugar, beat only until combined. Add eggs 1 at a time, beating only until ingredients are combined between additions. Stir creamed mixture into fruit mixture. Mix in sifted dry ingredients. Spread mixture into prepared pan, bake in slow oven 3 to 3½ hours. Brush top with extra rum, cover pan with foil, cool in pan overnight.

■ Cake can be made 6 months ahead.
■ Storage: Airtight container.
■ Freeze: Suitable.
■ Microwave: Not suitable.

RIGHT AND ABOVE: Rich Fruit Cake.
ABOVE RIGHT: Rock Cakes.
FAR RIGHT: Rocky Road.

Right: Tray and knife from Whitehill Silver & Plate; glasses from Bohemia Crystal.

Rock Cakes

2 cups self-raising flour
¼ teaspoon ground cinnamon
90g butter
⅓ cup caster sugar
1 cup (160g) sultanas
2 tablespoons mixed peel
1 egg, lightly beaten
½ cup milk, approximately
1 tablespoon caster sugar, extra

Sift flour and cinnamon into large bowl, rub in butter, stir in sugar and fruit. Stir in egg, then enough milk to give a moist but still firm consistency. Place 2 level tablespoons of mixture onto lightly greased oven trays about 5cm apart.

Sprinkle cakes with a little extra sugar. Bake in moderately hot oven about 15 minutes or until browned. Loosen cakes; cool on trays.
Makes about 18.

■ Cakes can be made up to 3 days ahead.
■ Storage: Airtight container.
■ Freeze: Suitable.
■ Microwave: Not suitable.

Rocky Road

The commercial variety of Rocky Road has been made for more than 40 years in Australia by Darrell Lea, who personalised their version by calling it Rocklea Road.

5 teaspoons gelatine
½ cup water
1 cup caster sugar
⅓ cup water, extra
2 teaspoons lemon juice
1 teaspoon vanilla essence
pink food colouring
⅓ cup coconut
375g milk chocolate, chopped
30g Copha, chopped
½ cup red glace cherries
½ cup unsalted roasted peanuts

Grease 2 x 8cm x 26cm bar pans.

Sprinkle gelatine over water in small bowl. Place sugar and extra water in medium pan, stir over heat, without boiling, until sugar is dissolved. Stir in gelatine mixture, bring to the boil; boil, without stirring, 8 minutes. Remove from heat, stir in juice and essence. Divide mixture into 2 small bowls; cool.

Tint 1 bowl of mixture pink. Beat each mixture with electric mixer until thick and holding its own shape. Spread mixtures into prepared pans, refrigerate about 1 hour or until set.

Sprinkle coconut over board, turn marshmallow from pans onto board, toss in coconut. Using a hot knife, cut marshmallow into squares.

Lightly grease 20cm x 30cm lamington pan, line with strip of foil to cover base and extend over 2 opposite ends.

Combine chocolate and Copha in heatproof bowl, stir over pan of simmering water until smooth; remove from heat, stand 10 minutes. Thinly spread ¼ cup of chocolate mixture over base of prepared pan. Place marshmallows and remaining coconut in pan, sprinkle with cherries and peanuts. Drizzle remaining chocolate evenly over mixture in pan. Refrigerate until set before cutting.

■ Recipe can be made a week ahead.
■ Storage: Covered, in refrigerator.
■ Freeze: Not suitable.
■ Microwave: Not suitable.

Rum Baba

It is thought that King Leszczynski of Poland invented the earliest version of this recipe in 1609 when he sprinkled some rum on a Kugelhupf, a rather dry yeast cake from Alsace. Apparently he named it Ali Baba after his favourite literary character.

15g compressed yeast
¼ cup plain flour
¼ cup warm milk
¾ cup plain flour, extra
2 tablespoons caster sugar
2 eggs, lightly beaten
60g butter, melted
RUM SYRUP
1½ cups caster sugar
1 cup water
2 tablespoons dark rum

Grease 6 moulds (½ cup capacity). Cream yeast with flour and milk in small bowl; cover, stand in warm place about 10 minutes, or until mixture is frothy.

Sift extra flour and sugar into large bowl, stir in yeast mixture, eggs and butter, beat about 3 minutes with wooden spoon until batter is smooth. Place batter into large greased bowl, cover, stand in warm place about 40 minutes, or until batter has doubled in size.

Beat batter again; divide batter between prepared moulds, stand, uncovered, until batter rises three-quarters of the way up side of moulds. Place moulds on oven tray, bake in moderately hot oven about 15 minutes. Cover tops if beginning to darken too much.

Turn babas onto wire rack over tray, pour hot rum syrup over hot babas. Place babas in serving plates, pour syrup from tray over babas until all syrup has been absorbed.

Rum Syrup: Combine sugar and water in pan, stir over heat, without boiling, until sugar is dissolved. Bring to boil; boil, uncovered, without stirring, 2 minutes. Remove from heat, stir in rum. Makes 6.

■ Recipe can be made a day ahead.
■ Storage: Airtight container.
■ Freeze: Suitable without syrup.
■ Microwave: Not suitable.

Rum Balls

4 cups (400g) fine cake crumbs
¼ cup cocoa
¼ cup apricot jam, warmed
2 tablespoons dark rum
2 tablespoons water
⅔ cup chocolate sprinkles

Combine crumbs and sifted cocoa in bowl; stir in combined strained jam, rum and water.

Roll 2 level teaspoons of mixture into balls. Roll balls in chocolate sprinkles. Refrigerate 2 hours before serving.
Makes about 45.

■ Recipe can be made a week ahead.
■ Storage: Covered, in refrigerator.
■ Freeze: Not suitable.

LEFT: Rum Baba.
RIGHT: From back: Rum Balls, Russian Caramels.

Left: Spoon from Whitehill Silver & Plate; fabric from Redelman & Son. Right: China from Noritake; tray from Oneida Silverware.

Russian Caramels

These require careful watching and constant whisking during cooking for scrumptious success.

125g butter
400g can sweetened condensed milk
2 tablespoons golden syrup
¾ cup brown sugar, firmly packed

Line deep 19cm square cake pan with foil, grease foil.

Combine all ingredients in heavy-based pan, stir over heat, without boiling, until butter has melted and sugar dissolved. Bring mixture to the boil, whisk constantly about 8 minutes or until mixture is thick and dark caramel in colour. Pour mixture into prepared pan. Stand caramel 20 minutes, mark into squares with greased knife; cool. Refrigerate caramel 1 hour before removing from pan.

■ Recipe can be made 1 week ahead.
■ Storage: Covered, in refrigerator.
■ Freeze: Not suitable.
■ Microwave: Not suitable.

Sago Steamed Pudding

Sago, like tapioca, is a starch used to make puddings and to thicken soups. Sago is obtained from the interior trunk of certain palm trees, while tapioca comes from the fleshy root of cassava or manioc. Sometimes sago is referred to as seed tapioca.

½ cup sago
2 cups milk
60g butter
1 teaspoon grated lemon rind
2 cups (400g) brown sugar, firmly packed
2 eggs, lightly beaten
2 cups (380g) dried mixed fruit
4 cups (280g) stale breadcrumbs
½ teaspoon bicarbonate of soda
2 teaspoons mixed spice

Grease pudding steamer (8 cup capacity). Combine sago and milk in small bowl, stand 1 hour.

Beat butter, rind, sugar and eggs in small bowl with electric mixer until light and creamy. Transfer mixture to large bowl, stir in sago mixture, fruit, breadcrumbs, sifted soda and spice; mix well. Pour mixture into prepared steamer, cover with greased foil, secure with string, cover with lid. Place steamer in boiler with enough boiling water to come halfway up side of steamer. Cover, boil about 4 hours. Replenish water when necessary. Serve with custard, if desired.
Serves 8.

■ Pudding can be made 4 days ahead.
■ Storage: Covered, in refrigerator.
■ Freeze: Suitable.
■ Microwave: Not suitable.

BELOW: Sago Steamed Pudding.
RIGHT: Sand Cake.
BELOW RIGHT: From left: Date Scones, Plain Scones.

Sand Cake

This cake is named for its slightly gritty or sandy texture which is a feature of cakes and shortbreads baked with rice flour. Using the coarser ground rice intensifies this texture.

180g butter
1 teaspoons vanilla essence
¾ cup caster sugar
3 eggs
½ cup self-raising flour
⅓ cup cornflour
⅓ cup rice flour or ground rice
2 tablespoons flaked almonds

Grease 20cm ring cake pan, line base with paper, grease paper.

Beat butter, essence and sugar in small bowl with electric mixer until light and fluffy. Add eggs 1 at a time, beating well between additions. Transfer mixture to large bowl, fold in sifted flours. Spread mixture into prepared pan, sprinkle with almonds. Bake in moderate oven about 40 minutes. Stand cake 5 minutes before turning onto wire rack to cool.

■ Cake can be made 4 days ahead.
■ Storage: Airtight container.
■ Freeze: Suitable.
■ Microwave: Not suitable.

Scones

Scones have been enjoyed for hundreds of years. The name probably comes from the Middle Dutch schoon brot, meaning fine bread. It has also been suggested that they were named after Scone, where Scottish kings used to be crowned.

The secret to good light scones is in the soft sticky dough, a light touch and a very hot oven.

2 cups self-raising flour
2 teaspoons caster sugar
15g butter
1 cup milk, approximately

Lightly grease 20cm round sandwich pan. Sift flour and sugar into bowl, rub in butter, stir in enough milk to mix to a soft sticky dough. Turn dough onto lightly floured surface, knead lightly until smooth. Press dough out to about 2cm thickness, cut into 5cm rounds. Place scones in prepared pan. Brush scones with a little extra milk. Bake in very hot oven about 15 minutes.
Makes about 10.
VARIATIONS
Date: Add 1 cup finely chopped dates to flour mixture.
Wholemeal: Substitute 1 cup wholemeal self-raising flour for 1 cup of the white self-raising flour.
■ Recipe best made just before serving.
■ Freeze: Suitable.
■ Microwave: Not suitable.

Scottish Black Bun

This is a traditional New Year, or Hogmanay bun. It is often brought to the house as a good luck gift by the first visitors to cross the threshold in the New Year, a ceremony known as 'first footing'. (It is thought particularly lucky if the very first person to visit is a tall, dark stranger.) Originally, the pastry was just a means of containing the rich, fruity mixture, rather like the sheeps' stomach of the famous haggis.

3 cups plain flour
250g butter
1 egg yolk
⅓ cup water, approximately
1 egg yolk, extra
1 tablespoon water, extra

FILLING
3⅓ cups (500g) currants
3 cups (500g) raisins, chopped
⅓ cup mixed peel
¾ cup almond kernels, chopped
½ cup whisky
½ cup brown sugar, firmly packed
½ cup milk
3 eggs, lightly beaten
¼ teaspoon finely ground
  black pepper
1½ cups plain flour
1½ teaspoons ground ginger
1½ teaspoons ground cinnamon
1½ teaspoons mixed spice

Lightly grease 14cm x 21cm loaf pan.

Sift flour into bowl, rub in butter. Add egg yolk and enough water to mix to a firm dough. Press dough into a ball, knead gently on lightly floured surface until smooth; cover, refrigerate 30 minutes.

Roll two-thirds of pastry on lightly floured surface, large enough to line base and sides of prepared pan. Gently ease pastry into pan; do not break or stretch pastry. Allow 1cm of pastry to overhang sides of pan. Press filling firmly into pastry case, level top. Roll remaining pastry into rectangle 1cm larger that the top of pan. Brush edges of pastry with combined extra egg yolk and extra water, top with rectangle of pastry, pinch edges together. Brush pastry with more egg yolk mixture. Bake in slow oven about 3¼ hours or until pastry is well browned; cool in pan.

To remove bun from pan, stand pan in hot water about 1 minute, carefully remove bun.

Filling: Combine all ingredients in large bowl, mix well.

■ Recipe can be made a month ahead.
■ Storage: Airtight container.
■ Freeze: Suitable.
■ Microwave: Not suitable.

Scottish Shortbread

Originally another Hogmanay specialty of Scotland, where it originated three or four hundred years ago, shortbread has become very popular in many parts of the globe and is now eaten all year.

250g butter
⅓ cup caster sugar
2 cups plain flour
½ cup rice flour or ground rice

Have butter at room temperature. Beat butter and sugar in small bowl with electric mixer until combined. Add large spoonfuls of sifted flours to butter mixture, beating between additions. Press ingredients together gently, knead on lightly floured surface until smooth.

Divide dough into 2 portions. Shape portions into 18cm rounds; place on greased oven trays, mark into wedges, prick with fork. Pinch a decorative edge with floured fingers. Bake in slow oven about 30 minutes. Stand 10 minutes before transferring to wire rack to cool. Cut when cold.
Makes 2.
■ Recipe can be made a month ahead.
■ Storage: Airtight container.
■ Freeze: Suitable.
■ Microwave: Not suitable.

Seed Cake, Caraway

180g butter
⅔ cup caster sugar
3 eggs
1 tablespoon caraway seeds
1½ cups self-raising flour
¼ cup milk

Grease 14cm x 21cm loaf pan. Beat butter and sugar in small bowl with electric mixer until light and fluffy; beat in eggs 1 at a time, beat until combined. Transfer mixture to large bowl, stir in seed, sifted flour and milk. Spread mixture into prepared pan, bake in moderate oven about 1 hour.
■ Recipe can be made 2 days ahead.
■ Storage: Airtight container.
■ Freeze: Suitable.
■ Microwave: Not suitable.

Seed Cake, Poppy

⅓ cup poppy seeds
¾ cup milk
180g butter, softened
2 teaspoons vanilla essence
1 cup caster sugar
3 eggs, lightly beaten
2 cups self-raising flour

Grease 14cm x 21cm loaf pan, line base with paper, grease paper. Combine poppy seeds and milk in medium bowl; cover, stand 1 hour.

Add butter, essence, sugar, eggs and sifted flour to poppy seed mixture; beat mixture on low speed with electric mixer until combined; beat on medium speed for about 3 minutes or until mixture is slightly changed in colour. Pour into prepared pan, bake in moderate oven about 1 hour. Stand in pan 5 minutes before turning onto wire rack to cool.
■ Recipe can be made a day ahead
■ Storage: Airtight container.
■ Freeze: Suitable.
■ Microwave: Not suitable.

LEFT: From left: Scottish Black Bun, Scottish Shortbread.
ABOVE: Seed Cakes, from left: Caraway, Poppy.

Snow Eggs

This splendid meringue and custard dessert is also known as Floating Islands or Oeufs a la Neige. It is an adaptation of a French pudding, Ile Flottante (Floating Island), which was made by floating a stale round sponge cake, steeped in liqueur and layered with jam, almonds and currants, in a bowl of custard.

**4 eggs, separated
1 cup caster sugar
2 cups milk
⅓ cup caster sugar, extra
2 teaspoons vanilla essence**

CARAMEL TOPPING
**½ cup sugar
¼ cup water**

Beat whites in small bowl with electric mixer until soft peaks form; gradually add sugar, beating until dissolved between additions. Combine milk, extra sugar and essence in shallow pan, stir until sugar has dissolved, bring to boil, remove from heat.

Working quickly, shape egg white mixture with 2 dessertspoons into egg shapes, drop shapes into scalded milk, leave 2 minutes. Turn shapes carefully with fork, leave in milk further 2 minutes. Remove shapes from milk with slotted spoon, drain on tray covered with absorbent paper. Repeat with remaining egg white mixture. Reheat milk to scalding between making each new batch of Snow Eggs.

Strain milk through fine sieve, return milk to pan, whisk in egg yolks; return to heat, stir over heat, without boiling, until mixture thickens slightly. Pour custard into serving dishes, top with snow eggs, drizzle with caramel topping.

Caramel Topping: Combine sugar and water in pan, stir over heat, without boiling, until sugar is dissolved. Boil, without stirring, until syrup is caramel coloured. Serves 4 to 6.

■ Recipe best made just before serving.
■ Freeze: Not suitable.
■ Microwave: Not suitable.

*LEFT: Snow Eggs.
RIGHT: Soda Bread.*

Left: Fabric from Redelman & Son. Right: Cabinet from Country Furniture Antiques.

Soda Bread

This famous Irish yeastless bread was originally made with plain flour, bicarbonate of soda and cream of tartar. The substitution of self-raising flour, and the interaction of the soda with the buttermilk, give this version its special texture and taste.

1½ cups plain flour
¾ cup self-raising flour
½ teaspoon salt
1 teaspoon bicarbonate of soda
60g butter
2 tablespoons caster sugar
1 egg, lightly beaten
¾ cup buttermilk

Sift flours, salt and soda into bowl, rub in butter, stir in sugar. Beat egg with 2 tablespoons of the buttermilk, reserve a little for glazing. Add remaining egg mixture to dry ingredients with enough milk to make ingredients cling together. Turn dough onto lightly floured surface, knead until smooth. Place dough on lightly greased oven tray. Press dough into 20cm round, cut a deep cross in top of dough. Brush with reserved egg mixture. Bake in moderately hot oven about 40 minutes.

VARIATION

Wholemeal: Substitute plain wholemeal flour for plain white flour. Sprinkle top with a mixture of seasame seeds and rolled oats, if desired.

■ Recipe best made on day of serving.
■ Freeze: Suitable.
■ Microwave: Not suitable.

Spanish Cream

This is a delicious adaptation of the popular Spanish baked custard known as Creme Caramel.
It is correct that the mixture separates.

2 eggs, separated
½ cup caster sugar
2 teaspoons vanilla essence
2 cups milk
2 tablespoons gelatine
⅓ cup hot water

Whisk egg yolks, sugar and essence in large pan until creamy, whisk in milk. Stir over heat, without boiling, until sugar is dissolved; bring to boil, remove from heat. Sprinkle gelatine over hot water, stir into milk mixture.

Beat egg whites in small bowl with electric mixer until firm peaks form. Fold whites into milk mixture in 2 batches. Pour into wetted mould (4 cup capacity), or into 4 individual dishes (1 cup capacity), refrigerate until firm.
Serves 4.

■ Recipe can be made 2 days ahead.
■ Storage: Covered, in refrigerator.
■ Freeze: Not suitable.
■ Microwave: Not suitable.

Sponge Fingers

Sponge Fingers, or Lady Fingers, are often used in charlotte russe.

½ cup caster sugar
2 eggs
1 cup plain flour

Lightly grease 2 oven trays or 1½ x 12-hole eclair tins. Place sugar in shallow ovenproof dish, place in moderate oven about 4 minutes or until sugar feels hot.

Beat eggs in small bowl with electric mixer until thick, gradually add hot sugar, continue beating until sugar is dissolved.

Meanwhile, triple sift flour. Transfer egg mixture to large bowl, sift flour over egg mixture, lightly fold in flour. Spoon mixture into piping bag fitted with 1½cm plain tube. Pipe mixture onto prepared trays in 8cm lengths (3cm wide) about 4cm apart; sprinkle with a little extra sugar. Bake 1 tray at a time in moderately hot oven about 8 minutes or until sponge fingers are lightly browned; cool on trays.
Makes about 18.

■ Recipe can be made a week ahead.
■ Storage: Airtight container.
■ Freeze: Not suitable.
■ Microwave: Not suitable.

Stollen

This yeast bread, traditionally served at Christmas, comes from Dresden in Germany.

1 cup (170g) raisins, chopped
¼ cup dark rum
60g compressed yeast
½ cup caster sugar
½ cup warm milk
4 cups (600g) plain flour
1 teaspoon ground cinnamon
250g butter, melted
⅓ cup mixed peel
⅔ cup blanched almonds
1 teaspoon grated lemon rind
200g roll marzipan
60g butter, melted, extra
icing sugar

Combine raisins and rum in bowl, cover, stand 30 minutes.

Cream yeast with 1 tablespoon of the caster sugar in small bowl, stir in milk; cover, stand in warm place about 10 minutes or until mixture is frothy.

Sift flour and cinnamon into large bowl, mix in remaining caster sugar. Stir in yeast mixture and butter, mix to a firm dough. Turn dough onto lightly floured surface, knead about 5 minutes or until dough is smooth and elastic. Return dough to large greased bowl, cover, stand in warm place about 30 minutes or until dough is doubled in size.

Turn dough onto lightly floured sur-face, knead in raisin mixture, peel, nuts and rind. Divide dough into 2 portions; shape each portion into a 22cm round. Divide marzipan into 2 portions, roll each portion into a sausage-shaped roll, the same length as the dough. Place roll just off centre on dough, fold dough almost in half, flatten slightly with hand. Place onto lightly greased oven trays, stand, covered, in warm place about 20 minutes or until stollen have increased in size by half. Brush stollen with extra butter.

Bake stollen in moderate oven about 35 minutes. Dust with sifted icing sugar before serving warm or cold.
Makes 2.
■ Stollen can be made a week ahead.
■ Storage: Airtight container.
■ Freeze: Suitable.
■ Microwave: Not suitable.

LEFT: Sponge Fingers.
BELOW LEFT: Spanish Cream.
BELOW: Stollen.

Below: Embroidered cloth from F. Alexander.

Strawberries Romanoff

The exact origin of this dish appears lost in time; it was presumably invented for one of the famous Romanovs, either by one of their chefs or by a Paris restaurant.

2 x 250g punnets strawberries, halved
1½ tablespoons Kirsch
2 teaspoons icing sugar
2 tablespoons icing sugar, extra
½ cup thickened cream
pink food colouring

Combine berries, liqueur and icing sugar in bowl, refrigerate 30 minutes. Drain berries, reserve liquid. Divide three-quarters of the berries into 4 dishes. Blend or process remaining berries, extra icing sugar and reserved liquid until smooth. Beat cream until soft peaks form, fold in berry mixture, tint pink with colouring.

Serve cream mixture over berries. Decorate with extra berries, if desired. Serves 4.

■ Recipe can be prepared 2 hours before serving.
■ Storage: Refrigerator.
■ Freeze: Not suitable.

Strawberry Shortcake

Although most people would associate this dish with America, the shortcake in fact originated in England and Europe. In England it was known as shortbread, until that name came to be used almost exclusively for the Scottish New Year shortbreads. The American version uses a scone-like dough and is usually served with lashings of whipped cream.

250g butter
1 teaspoon grated lemon rind
1 tablespoon lemon juice
½ cup caster sugar
⅓ cup rice flour or ground rice
1 cup self-raising flour
1⅓ cups plain flour
250g punnet strawberries, halved
½ cup strawberry jam

Lightly grease 26cm recessed flan tin. Have butter at room temperature.

Beat butter, rind, juice and sugar in small bowl with electric mixer until creamy. Stir in sifted flours in 2 batches. Press ingredients together gently, knead lightly until smooth. Press evenly into prepared tin. Bake in moderate oven about 20 minutes or until lightly browned; cool in tin.

Turn shortcake onto serving plate, decorate with berries. Warm jam in small pan, strain, brush evenly oven berries.

■ Shortcake can be made a week ahead; assemble just before serving.
■ Storage: Covered, in refrigerator.
■ Freeze: Shortcake suitable.
■ Microwave: Jam suitable.

Streusel Coffee Cake

Originally from Bohemia, in Czechoslovakia, this delicious cake has since been adopted as their own by the cooks of Vienna, Germany and Alsace, among other places.

The topping, which has a good buttery texture, should be made first.

180g butter
2 teaspoons vanilla essence
1 cup caster sugar
3 eggs
1½ cups self-raising flour
¾ cup plain flour
½ cup sour cream

TOPPING

¾ cup plain flour
3 teaspoons ground cinnamon
60g butter
⅓ cup brown sugar

Grease 20cm x 30cm lamington pan. Have butter for cake at room temperature. Beat butter, essence and sugar in small bowl with electric mixer until light and fluffy; beat in eggs 1 at a time, beat until combined. Transfer mixture to large bowl, stir in sifted flours and cream. Spread mixture into prepared pan. Coarsely grate topping over cake, bake in moderate oven about 35 minutes. Stand cake 5 minutes before turning onto wire rack to cool.

Topping: Sift flour and cinnamon into bowl, rub in butter, stir in sugar. Press mixture into a ball, cover, freeze about 30 minutes or until firm.

■ Recipe can be made 2 days ahead.
■ Storage: Airtight container.
■ Freeze: Suitable.
■ Microwave: Not suitable.

Sultana Cake

3 cups (500g) sultanas
250g butter
¾ cup caster sugar
5 eggs
2½ cups plain flour
¼ cup self-raising flour
¼ cup brandy

Grease 23cm round cake pan, line base with paper, grease paper. Place sultanas in bowl, add enough hot water to cover; cover bowl, stand 2 hours.

Drains sultanas, spread sultanas on tray covered with absorbent paper or tea towel; cover, stand overnight.

Have butter at room temperature. Beat butter and sugar in small bowl with electric mixer until light and fluffy; beat in eggs 1 at a time, beat until combined. Transfer mixture to large bowl, stir in sifted flours, sultanas and brandy in 2 batches. Spread into prepared pan, bake in moderately slow oven about 1¾ hours. Cover cake, cool in pan.

■ Cake can be made a week ahead.
■ Storage: Airtight container.
■ Freeze: Suitable.
■ Microwave: Not suitable.

LEFT: From left: Strawberry Shortcake, Strawberries Romanoff.
ABOVE: From left: Streusel Cake, Sultana Cake.

Left: Glasses and bowl from Bohemia Crystal.
Above: China from Noritake.

Summer Pudding

The classic British summer pudding, made with raspberries and redcurrants, could only be made for a brief period in mid-summer, when both fruits were ripe. Equally lovely versions were made, especially by country people, with other berries in season, including blackberries and wild bilberries. The advent of freezing means this dessert can now be enjoyed all year. Use berries of your choice.

250g frozen raspberries
250g frozen strawberries
250g frozen boysenberries
¾ cup caster sugar
1 cup water
10 slices 2 day old white bread

Combine berries in bowl, thaw to room temperature. Drain berries, reserve juice.

Combine reserved berry juice, sugar and water in small pan, stir over heat, without boiling, until sugar is dissolved; bring to boil, simmer, uncovered, with-

out stirring, for 2 minutes.

Remove crusts from bread, cut bread to fit base and side of glass bowl (5 cup capacity). Spread half the fruit mixture into bowl. Pour quarter of sugar syrup over fruit. Cover with a layer of bread. Repeat layering with remaining

fruit and bread, finishing with bread.

Pour remaining syrup down side of bowl and evenly over top. Stand 20 minutes to allow bread to absorb syrup. Cover surface of pudding with plastic wrap, put a heavy weight on top, refrigerate overnight. As pudding flattens, decrease size of weight to fit into shape of bowl. Turn pudding onto serving plate, spoon any syrup over pudding. Serve with whipped cream, if desired. Serves 6 to 8.

■ Recipe can be made 2 days ahead.
■ Storage: Covered, in refrigerator.
■ Freeze: Not suitable.
■ Microwave: Syrup suitable.

Swiss Roll

Also know as Jam Roll, or Jelly Roll in the United States, this has long been a favourite British cake, although its origins seem obscure. It can also be rolled with a cream filling.

3 eggs, separated
½ cup caster sugar
¾ cup self-raising flour
2 tablespoons hot milk
caster sugar, extra
½ cup jam, warmed

Grease 26cm x 32cm Swiss roll pan, line base and sides with paper, grease paper.

Beat egg whites in small bowl with electric mixer until soft peaks form; gradually add sugar, beating until dissolved between additions. Add yolks 1 at a time, beating well until thick and light. Fold in triple sifted flour and milk. Pour mixture into prepared pan, bake in hot oven about 8 minutes.

Meanwhile, place a sheet of paper same size as sponge on bench, sprinkle lightly with some extra caster sugar. When sponge is cooked, turn immediately onto paper, quickly peel away lining paper. Cut off crisp edge from long sides, spread sponge evenly with jam, commence rolling from short side with help of paper. Lift sponge onto wire rack to cool.

■ Recipe best made on day of serving.
■ Freeze: Suitable.
■ Microwave: Jam suitable.

LEFT: Summer Pudding.
ABOVE: Swiss Roll.

Syllabub

In Elizabethan England, frothing milk was mixed with wine or cider to create this dish. Legend has it that the froth was achieved by milking the cow directly into the bowl of wine. Bub was the Elizabethan term for bubbling drink and Sille or Sillery, in France, was the source of England's best known wine.

Use fruit of your choice in this recipe.
½ cup dry white wine
2 teaspoons grated lemon rind
2 tablespoons lemon juice
½ cup caster sugar
300ml carton thickened cream
250g punnet strawberries, sliced

Combine wine, rind, juice and sugar in small bowl, stir until sugar is dissolved. Add cream, beat with electric mixer until soft peaks form. Divide berries between 6 glasses. Serve syllabub over berries; refrigerate 2 hours before serving. Serve syllabub wth extra berries and lemon rind, if desired.
Serves 6.

■ Recipe can be made a day ahead.
■ Freeze: Not suitable.

BELOW: Syllabub.
RIGHT: Tapioca Custard.

Tapioca Custard

Tapioca, like sago, is a starch used to made puddings and to thicken soups. Tapioca is obtained from the fleshy root of a tropical plant called cassava or manioc, while sago comes from the interior trunk of certain palm trees. Sometimes sago is referred to as seed tapioca.

½ cup tapioca
1 cup boiling water
¼ cup cold water
1 cup milk
3 eggs
1 teaspoon vanilla essence
¼ cup sugar

Combine tapioca and boiling water in small bowl; cover, stand overnight.

Combine tapioca mixture, cold water and milk in pan, stir over heat, without boiling, about 20 minutes or until mixture has thickened slightly and tapioca is opaque; cool 5 minutes. Whisk eggs, essence and sugar together in bowl; stir in tapioca mixture. Pour mixture into greased shallow ovenproof dish (4 cup capacity). Place dish into baking dish, add enough boiling water to come halfway up side of dish. Bake, uncovered, in moderate oven about 1 hour or until just set.
Serves 4.
◾ Recipe best made on day of serving.
◾ Storage: Covered, in refrigerator.
◾ Freeze: Not suitable.
◾ Microwave: Not suitable.

Tipsy Cake

Also known as Sussex Tipsy Cake, this popular old English cake is the trifle's early ancestor. Our recipe is very close to the original in that the sponge is soaked in brandy. Since the 19th century, white wine or sherry have more commonly been used.

20cm round sponge cake
⅔ cup madeira
1 tablespoon brandy
½ cup raspberry jam
300ml carton thickened cream, whipped

CREME ANGLAISE
4 egg yolks
1 teaspoon vanilla essence
2 tablespoons caster sugar
2 cups milk

Split sponge into 3 layers. Combine madeira and brandy in jug, brush generously over each layer. Sandwich cake layers with jam, place cake onto serving plate. Just before serving, cover cake all over with cream. Serve cake with creme anglaise. Decorate with strawberries, if desired.

Creme Anglaise: Whisk yolks, essence and sugar in heatproof bowl until pale and thick. Heat milk until almost boiling, gradually whisk into egg mixture. Place mixture over pan of simmering water, stir about 20 minutes or until custard has thickened slightly.

Serves 6.

■ Undecorated cake best assembled a day ahead.
■ Storage: Covered, in refrigerator.
■ Freeze: Not suitable.
■ Microwave: Not suitable.

Toffee Apples

You will need 10 thick wooden skewers for this recipe. They are available from some butchers or cake decorating suppliers.

10 small apples
4 cups sugar
1 cup water
⅓ cup glucose syrup
1 teaspoon red food colouring

LEFT: From left: Tipsy Cake, Tortoni.
RIGHT: Toffee Apples.

Left: Fabric from Redelman & Son; plate and glasses from Bohemia Crystal.

Rinse apples under cold water, stand on rack until completely dry; do not rub with a cloth. Push a skewer three-quarters of the way into each apple at stem end.

Combine sugar, water, glucose and colouring in heavy-based saucepan. Stir over heat, without boiling, until sugar is dissolved. Boil, uncovered, without stirring, about 20 minutes or until mixture reaches hard crack stage.

To test: Remove sugar syrup from heat, allow bubbles to subside. Drop a teaspoon of syrup into a cup of cold water. It should set hard and be hard to crack with fingers. Alternatively, the sugar syrup should reach 155°C when tested with a candy thermometer.

Remove syrup from heat, stand pan in baking dish of warm water about 1 minute or until bubbles subside. Remove pan from water, tilt pan, dip and rotate an apple slowly in toffee until apple is completely coated. Twirl apple round a few times before placing onto greased oven tray to set. Repeat with remaining apples and toffee.
Makes 10.
- Recipe best made on day of serving.
- Storage: Wrapped, airtight, in plastic wrap.
- Freeze: Not suitable.
- Microwave: Not suitable.

Tortoni

This Italian ice-cream is named after Signor Tortoni, who had a cafe in Paris around 1800.

Mix and match fruit, nuts and liqueur to suit your taste. Try glace apricots with pistachio nuts and Apricot Brandy, or glace pineapple, macadamia nuts and Malibu.

2 egg whites
2 tablespoons caster sugar
½ cup chopped glace cherries
⅔ cup slivered almonds, toasted
**300ml carton thickened cream,
    whipped**
1 tablespoon Cherry Brandy

Beat egg whites in small bowl with electric mixer until firm peaks form; add sugar gradually, beat until sugar is dissolved and mixture is thick and glossy. Fold in fruit, nuts, cream and liqueur. Spoon into 4 serving dishes (¾ cup capacity), cover, freeze until firm.
Serves 4.
- Recipe best made a day ahead.
- Storage: Covered, in freezer.
- Freeze: Suitable.

Treacle Tart

A hearty and very old English recipe that was once a feature of restaurant and cafe menus. Its American cousin is known as Molasses Pie.

1¼ cups plain flour
⅓ cup custard powder
2 tablespoons icing sugar
125g butter, chopped
2 tablespoons milk, approximately

FILLING
1½ cups (100g) stale breadcrumbs
1 cup treacle
2 teaspoons grated lemon rind

Sift flour, custard powder and icing sugar into medium bowl, rub in butter. Add enough milk to make ingredients cling together. Press dough into ball, knead gently on lightly floured surface until smooth; cover, refrigerate 30 minutes.

Roll two-thirds of dough large enough to line 22cm flan tin. Lift pastry into tin, gently ease into side, trim edge. Place tin on oven tray, line pastry with paper, fill with dried beans or rice. Bake in moderately hot oven 10 minutes; remove paper and beans, bake further 10 minutes or until lightly browned; cool.

Spread filling into pastry case. Roll remaining pastry into a rectangle on lightly floured surface; cut into 1cm strips. Brush edge of pastry case lightly with a little extra milk. Place pastry strips over filling in lattice pattern, brush pastry lightly with a little more milk. Bake in moderate oven about 25 minutes or until pastry is lightly browned. Cool tart in pan. Sprinkle with a little icing sugar before serving. Serve with whipped cream or ice-cream.

Filling: Combine all ingredients in bowl; mix well.

Serves 6 to 8.

■ Recipe can be made a day ahead.
■ Storage: Covered, in refrigerator.
■ Freeze: Suitable.
■ Microwave: Not suitable.

Trifle

Probably the best loved of English cold puddings, the trifle has a long and distinguished history, related to the Tipsy Cake. Although it is sometimes regarded as a good way to use up 'leftovers', it was originally a magnificent dish in its own right, using rich ingredients in complex compositions.

100g packet strawberry jelly crystals
300g jam sponge roll
¼ cup sherry
425g can sliced peaches, drained
300ml carton thickened cream, whipped

CUSTARD
2 tablespoons custard powder
2 tablespoons caster sugar
2 cups milk
1 teaspoon vanilla essence

Make jelly according to directions on packet, refrigerate until jelly is just beginning to set.

Cut sponge roll into 1cm slices, place over base and around side of large glass serving bowl, sprinkle with sherry. Pour partly set jelly over sponge roll, refrigerate until jelly is set. Place peaches over jelly, spread evenly with custard, top with cream; refrigerate. Decorate with fresh fruit or grated chocolate, if desired.

Custard: Blend custard powder and sugar with a little of the milk in pan, stir in remaining milk. Stir over heat until custard boils and thickens. Remove from heat, stir in essence; cover, cool.

Serves 6 to 8.

■ Recipe best made a day ahead.
■ Storage: Covered, in refrigerator.
■ Freeze: Not suitable.
■ Microwave: Custard suitable.

LEFT: Treacle Tart.
RIGHT: Trifle.

Twelfth Night Cake

Originally a pagan festival, Twelfth Night was taken over by the Church in the 4th century. It was a special festive night, falling at the end of Christmas celebrations. A bean was cooked in the cake, and whoever found it was king or queen for the night.

250g butter
1 teaspoon vanilla essence
1 cup caster sugar
4 eggs
⅓ cup sliced glace cherries
½ cup sultanas
⅓ cup finely chopped dried apricots
1 cup (90g) packaged ground almonds
1 cup plain flour
¾ cup self-raising flour
½ teaspoon ground cinnamon
¼ cup milk

Grease deep 20cm round cake pan, line base with paper, grease paper.

Beat butter, essence and sugar in small bowl with electric mixer until light and fluffy. Add eggs 1 at a time, beating well between additions. Transfer mixture to large bowl, stir in fruit and nuts, then sifted dry ingredients alternately with milk. Spread mixture into prepared pan, bake in slow oven about 2 hours. Cover cake with foil, cool in pan.

■ Recipe can be made a week ahead.
■ Storage: Airtight container.
■ Freeze: Suitable.
■ Microwave: Not suitable.

BELOW: Twelfth Night Cake.

Vanilla Ice-Cream

Iced concoctions have a long history indeed. A very early version consisted of flavoured snow, which the Romans are said to have enjoyed. The Italians continued to develop ice-cream, introducing it to France where it became popular more than 100 years ago.

Shallow pans should be used for the freezing stages of ice-cream to freeze it faster, lessening crystal formation.

¾ cup caster sugar
4cm piece vanilla bean, split
3 x 300ml cartons thickened cream

Line a lamington pan with plastic wrap, leave wrap overhanging edges. This makes it easier to remove the ice-cream for beating.

Combine sugar, vanilla bean and 1 carton of the cream in pan, stir over heat, without boiling, until sugar is dissolved. Remove from heat, stir in remaining cream; remove vanilla bean. Strain mixture through fine cloth into prepared pan, cover; freeze 3 hours or until just firm.

Spoon mixture into large bowl, beat with electric mixer until smooth and creamy. Return to lined pan, cover, freeze 3 hours, or until just firm. Repeat beating once more, return to pan, cover, freeze 3 hours or overnight.
Makes about 1 litre.

■ Recipe can be made a week ahead.
■ Storage: Covered, in freezer.
■ Microwave: Cream mixture suitable.

BELOW: Vanilla Ice-Cream served on Waffles with Caramel Sauce. (Recipe for Waffles with Caramel Sauce is on page 120.)

Vanilla Slice

A long-time favourite in cake shops, canteens and takeaway food outlets.

2 sheets ready-rolled puff pastry
1 cup caster sugar
¾ cup cornflour
½ cup custard powder
1 litre (4 cups) milk
60g butter
2 egg yolks, lightly beaten
2 teaspoons vanilla essence

PASSIONFRUIT ICING

2 cups icing sugar
1 teaspoon soft butter
2 tablespoons passionfruit pulp, strained
2 teaspoons water, approximately

Line 23cm square slab pan with foil, bring foil up to overlap sides of pan.

Place pastry sheets on lightly greased oven trays, bake in hot oven about 6 minutes or until well browned; cool. Gently flatten pastry with hand, fit 1 pastry sheet in prepared pan.

Combine sugar, conflour and custard powder in pan, gradually stir in milk, stir until smooth. Add butter, stir over heat until mixture boils and thickens; simmer, stirring about 3 minutes or until very thick and smooth. Remove from heat, stir in yolks and essence. Pour hot custard over pastry in pan, top with remaining sheet of pastry, flat side up. Press down slightly; cool. Spread pastry with passionfruit icing. Cut when set.

Passionfruit Icing: Sift icing sugar into small heatproof bowl; stir in butter, passionfruit juice and enough water to make a stiff paste. Stir icing over hot water until spreadable.

■ Recipe can be made a day ahead.
■ Storage: Covered, in refrigerator.
■ Freeze: Not suitable.
■ Microwave: Not suitable.

Victoria Sandwich

Among the many memorials to Queen Victoria, which include fountains, statues and states, are several culinary creations. The Victoria Sandwich is undoubtedly the best known.

250g butter
1 teaspoon vanilla essence
1 cup caster sugar
4 eggs
2 cups self-raising flour
2 tablespoons jam
icing sugar

Grease 2 deep 20cm round cake pans, cover bases with paper; grease paper.

Beat butter, essence and sugar in small bowl with electric mixer until mixture is light and fluffy. Add eggs 1 at a time, beat well between additions. Transfer to large bowl, stir in sifted flour in 2 batches. Spread mixture evenly between prepared pans. Bake in moderate oven for about 25 minutes.

Turn cakes onto wire rack to cool. Join cakes with jam, dust cake with a little sifted icing sugar.

■ Recipe best made on day of serving.
■ Freeze: Suitable.
■ Microwave: Not suitable.

LEFT: Vanilla Slice.
RIGHT: Victoria Sandwich.

Right: China from Mikasa.

Waffles with Caramel Sauce

Although waffles seem to be synonymous with America, they were in fact very popular in France more than 500 years ago. They were also well known in Germany and Holland. Our word for them derives form the German word wabe, meaning honeycomb, which the surface of a waffle resembles.

1¾ cups plain flour
¼ cup self-raising flour
¼ cup caster sugar
2 eggs, separated
1½ cups milk
60 butter, melted
2 tablespoons water

CARAMEL SAUCE
125g butter
1 cup (200g) brown sugar, firmly packed
300ml carton thickened cream

Sift flours and sugar into bowl; make well in centre, gradually stir in combined egg yolks and milk, then butter and water; stir until smooth. Beat egg whites in small bowl until soft peaks form, fold into mixture in 2 batches.

Drop about ⅓ cup mixture onto prepared waffle iron. Close iron, cook about 2 minutes or until waffle is golden brown. Repeat with remaining mixture. Serve the waffles immediately with caramel sauce.

Caramel Sauce: Melt butter in medium pan, add sugar, stir over heat, without boiling, until sugar is dissolved. Bring to boil, simmer, without stirring, 2 minutes. Remove from heat, allow bubbles to subside, stir in cream.

Makes 12 waffles, 1½ cups sauce.
- Waffles best made just before serving. Sauce can be made a day ahead.
- Storage: Sauce, covered, in refrigerator.
- Freeze: Not suitable.
- Microwave: Not suitable.

RIGHT: White Christmas.
FAR RIGHT: Yorkshire Curd Tarts.
(Waffles with Caramel Sauce pictured on page 117 with Vanilla Ice-Cream.)

Right: Plate from Gien; Christmas decorations from Albi Imports.

White Christmas

Copha is an Australian ingredient. See glossary for substitutes.
250g Copha
1 cup (40g) Rice Bubbles
1 cup (110g) full-cream milk powder
1 cup (90g) coconut
1 cup icing sugar
½ cup sultanas
⅓ cup halved red and green glace cherries
1 glace pinapple ring, chopped
2 glace apricots, chopped

Grease and line deep 19cm square cake pan. Melt Copha in pan over low heat. Combine all ingredients in bowl; mix well. Press mixture into prepared pan, cover, refrigerate until set. Remove from refrigerator 15 minutes before cutting.
- Recipe can be made a week ahead.
- Storage: Covered, in refrigerator.
- Freeze: Not suitable.
- Microwave: Copha suitable.

Yorkshire Curd Tarts

This recipe is a variation of Maids of Honour made with currants or raisins. In Yorkshire it is normally prepared as a large tart, known as Yorkshire Curd Cheesecake.

3 cups milk
2 tablespoons white vinegar
1 sheet ready-rolled puff pastry
1½ tablespoons apricot jam
¼ cup currants
2 tablespoons caster sugar
2 eggs, lightly beaten
1 teaspoon grated lemon rind

Combine milk and vinegar in pan; heat, stirring, until milk separates. Strain mixture through fine sieve, gently press excess liquid from curd; do not press curd through sieve. Discard liquid.

Roll pastry on lightly floured surface until very thin, to about 30cm x 50cm rectangle. Cut 6½cm rounds from pastry. Place pastry rounds in 2 ungreased 12-hole shallow patty pans.

Place ¼ teaspoon jam into each pastry case, sprinkle with ½ teaspoon currants. Place curd in bowl, stir in sugar, eggs and rind; mix well. Place about 2 level teaspoons of mixture into each pastry case. Bake in moderately hot oven about 15 minutes or until lightly browned. Stand 5 minutes before cooling on wire racks.

Makes 24.

■ Recipe can be made a day ahead.
■ Storage: Airtight container.
■ Freeze: Not suitable.
■ Microwave: Not suitable.

Zabaglione

Also known as Zabaione, this is a very old Italian recipe for a custard made with marsala, a sweet wine from Sicily. It was first created in Venice, but is now very popular all over the world.

4 egg yolks
¼ cup caster sugar
⅓ cup marsala

Beat egg yolks and sugar in small bowl with electric mixer until thick and creamy. Transfer mixture to medium heatproof bowl, place bowl over pan of simmering water; gradually beat in marsala, then beat mixture for about 10 minutes or until mixture is thick and creamy and will hold its own shape.
Serves 4.
■ Recipe best made just before serving.
■ Freeze: Not suitable.
■ Microwave: Not suitable.

RIGHT: Zabaglione

Right: Glass and spoon from Bohemia Crystal; fabric from Redelman & Son.

Glossary

Here are some terms, names and alternatives to help everyone use and understand our recipes perfectly.

ALCOHOL: is optional but gives a special flavour. You can use fruit juice or water instead to make up the liquid content of our recipes.

ALLSPICE: pimento in ground form.

ALMONDS:
Flaked: sliced almonds.
Ground: we used packaged commercially ground nuts, unless otherwise specified.
Slivered: almonds cut lengthways.

APPLES: we used Granny Smith apples in this book.

ARROWROOT: used mostly for thickening. Cornflour can be substituted.

BAKING PAPER: can be used to line cake pans, make piping bags, etc. It is not necessary to grease after lining pans, unless otherwise specified.

BAKING POWDER: is a raising agent consisting on an alkali and an acid. It is mostly made from cream of tartar and bicarbonate of soda in the proportion of 1 teaspoon of cream of tartar to ½ teaspoon bicarbonate of soda. This is equivalent to 2 teaspoons baking powder.

BICARBONATE OF SODA: also known as baking soda.

BISCUIT CRUMBS, SWEET: use any plain, sweet biscuits (cookies). Blend or process biscuits until finely and evenly crushed.

BREADCRUMBS:
Packaged dry: use fine packaged breadcrumbs.
Stale: use 1 or 2 day old white bread made into crumbs by grating, blending or processing.

BUTTER: use salted or unsalted (also called sweet) butter; 125g is equal to 1 stick butter.

BUTTERMILK: is now made by adding a culture to skim milk to give a slightly acid flavour; skim milk can be substituted, if preferred.

CACHOUS: small round cake-decorating sweets available in silver, gold or various colours. See picture above right.

CHEESE:
Cream: also known as Philly.
Ricotta: a fresh unripened light curd cheese with a rich flavour.

CHESTNUT SPREAD: available from delicatessens and some supermarkets; it is made from sweetened, flavoured, pureed chestnuts.

CHOCOLATE, DARK: we used a good quality cooking chocolate.

CHOC BITS (morsels): are small buds of dark chocolate available in 100g and 250g packets; these do not melt when cooked in biscuits and cakes. One cup will hold about 155g. See picture below.

Clockwise from bottom left: Coloured Nonpareils, Silver Cachous, Gold Cachous, Choc Bits, Chocolate Nonpareils.

COCOA: cocoa powder.

COCONUT: we used desiccated coconut, unless otherwise specified.
Essence: extract.
Flaked: flaked and dried coconut flesh.
Shredded: thin strips of dried coconut.

COPHA: a solid white shortening based on coconut oil. Kremelta and Palmin can be substituted.

CORN FLAKES: breakfast cereal made from toasted corn.

CORN SYRUP: an imported product available in light or dark varieties. Glucose syrup can be substituted.

CORNFLOUR: cornstarch.

CORNMEAL: ground corn (maize); is similar to polenta but pale yellow in colour and finer. One can be substituted for the other but the results will be slightly different.

CREAM: is light pouring cream, also known as half 'n' half.
Sour: a thick commercially cultured soured cream.
Sour Light: a less dense commercially cultured soured cream; do not substitute this for sour cream.

Thickened (whipping): is specified when necessary in recipes. Double cream or cream with more than 35 percent fat can be substituted.

CUSTARD POWDER: pudding mix.

ESSENCE: extract.

FLOUR:
Rice: flour made from rice; ground rice can be substituted.
White Plain: all-purpose flour.
White Self-Raising: substitute plain (all-purpose) flour and baking powder in the proportion of ¾ cup plain flour to 2 teaspoons of baking powder. Sift together several times before using. If using 8oz measuring cup use 1 cup plain flour to 2 teaspoons baking powder.
Wholemeal Plain: wholewheat all-purpose flour.
Wholemeal Self-Raising (wholewheat): substitute plain wholemeal flour and baking powder in the proportion of ¾ cup plain wholemeal flour to 2 teaspoons baking powder; sift together several times before using. If using an 8oz measuring cup use 1 cup plain wholemeal flour to 2 teaspoons baking powder.

FRUIT MINCE: is also known as mincemeat.

GINGER:
Glace: fresh ginger root preserved in sugar syrup; crystallised ginger can be substituted; rinse off sugar with warm water; dry ginger well before using.
Ground: is also available but should not be substituted for fresh ginger. See picture below.

Clockwise from bottom left: Crystallised Ginger, Fresh Ginger, Glace Ginger, Ground Ginger.

GLUCOSE SYRUP (liquid glucose): is clear with a consistency like honey; it is made from wheat starch; available at health food stores and supermarkets.

Do not confuse it with the powdered glucose drink.

GOLDEN SYRUP: maple, pancake syrup or honey can be substituted.
GRAND MARNIER: an orange-flavoured liqueur.
GREASEPROOF PAPER: we used this paper to line cake pans etc; do not confuse with the shiny wax paper. It is best to grease greaseproof paper after lining the pan. Baking paper can also be used for lining pans.
GROUND ALMONDS/HAZELNUTS: we used packaged commercially ground nuts unless otherwise specified.
GROUND RICE: rice flour can be substituted; it will give a finer texture than ground rice.
HUNDREDS AND THOUSANDS: nonpareils. See picture on previous page.
JAMS AND CONSERVES: a preservative of sugar and fruit.
JELLY CRYSTALS: fruit-flavoured gelatine crystals available from supermarkets.
KIRSCH: a cherry-flavoured liqueur.
LARD: the clean, white fat rendered from the meat of pigs.
LEMON BUTTER: lemon cheese or lemon curd.
LIQUEURS: we have used a variety of liqueurs: if desired, you can use brandy instead (however, the flavour will change). If alcohol is not desirable, substitute with fruit juice of an equivalent flavour or milk or water to balance the liquid proportions in the recipe.
MADEIRA: wine fortified with brandy.
MAPLE SYRUP: we used a good quality, imported maple syrup.
MARSALA: a sweet fortified wine.
MARZIPAN, ROLL: a smooth, firm confectionery paste.
MILK: we used full-cream homogenised milk, unless otherwise specified.
Evaporated: unsweetened canned milk from which water has been extracted.
Sweetened Condensed: we used Nestle's milk which has had 60 percent of the water removed, then sweetened with sugar.
MIXED DRIED FRUIT: a combination of sultanas, raisins, currants, mixed peel and cherries.
MIXED PEEL: a mixture of crystallised citrus peel; also known as candied peel.
MIXED SPICE: a blend of ground spices usually consisting of cinnamon, allspice and nutmeg.
OIL: polyunsaturated vegetable oil.
PUFF PASTRY, READY-ROLLED: frozen sheets of puff pastry available from supermarkets.
PUNNET: small basket usually holding about 250g fruit.
RICE BUBBLES: rice crispies.
RICE FLOUR: ground rice can be substituted for rice flour.
RIND: zest.
ROLLED OATS: processed cereal used to make porridge.
RUM, DARK: we prefer to use an underproof rum (not overproof) for a more subtle flavour.
SAGO: also sold as seed tapioca. Tapioca can be used as a substitute for sago; it will need more cooking. See picture below.

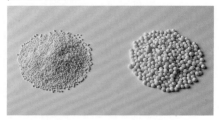

From left: Sago, Tapioca.

SUGAR: We used coarse granulated table sugar (also known as crystal sugar), unless otherwise specified.
Brown: a soft fine-granulated sugar with molasses present which gives it its characteristic colour.
Caster: fine granulated table sugar.
Demerara: small golden-coloured crystal sugar.
Icing: also known as confectioners' sugar or powdered sugar. We used icing sugar mixture, not pure icing sugar. See picture below.

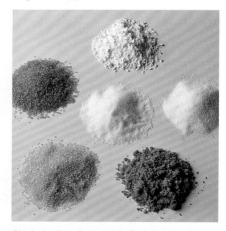

Clockwise from bottom left: Raw Sugar, Demerara Sugar, Icing Sugar, Caster Sugar, Brown Sugar, Crystal Sugar (centre).

SULTANAS: seedless white raisins.
TAPIOCA: balls of starch extracted from the roots of the cassava (manioc) plant. Resembles sago in appearance although tapioca balls are larger. See picture at left.
TREACLE: golden syrup or honey can be substituted.
VANILLA BEAN: dried bean of the vanilla orchid. Used as a flavouring for puddings, cakes, creams etc. It can be used repeatedly; simple wash in warm water after use, dry well and store in airtight container. See picture below.

From left: Whole Vanilla Bean, Split Vanilla Bean.

VANILLA ESSENCE: we used imitation vanilla extract.
WHISKY: we used a good quality scotch whisky.
WINE: we used good quality dry white and red wines.
YEAST: allow 2 teaspoons (7g) dried granulated yeast to each 15g compressed yeast.

Cake Pans

We tested a lot of the recipes in this book using Namco aluminium cake pans (see picture). If using pans which have a non-stick coating, or are anodised, or are made from stainless steel, or tin, best results will be obtained by reducing the oven temperature by 10° Celsius (25° Fahrenheit).

1. Deep 20cm round cake pan
2. 20cm round sandwich pan
3. Deep 23cm round cake pan
4. 20cm ring cake pan
5. 20cm x 30cm lamington pan
6. 23cm square slab pan
7. 26cm x 32cm Swiss roll pan

8. 15cm x 25cm loaf pan
9. 14cm x 21cm loaf pan
10. 8cm x 26cm bar cake pan
11. Deep 19cm square cake pan
12. 12-hole shallow patty pan
13. 12-hole deep patty pan
14. 21cm baba pan

FACTS AND FIGURES

Wherever you live, you'll be able to use our recipes with the help of these easy-to-follow conversions. While these conversions are approximate only, the difference between an exact and the approximate conversion of various liquid and dry measures is but minimal and will not affect your cooking results.

DRY MEASURES

Metric	Imperial
15g	½oz
30g	1oz
60g	2oz
90g	3oz
125g	4oz (¼lb)
155g	5oz
185g	6oz
220g	7oz
250g	8oz (½lb)
280g	9oz
315g	10oz
345g	11oz
375g	12oz (¾lb)
410g	13oz
440g	14oz
470g	15oz
500g	16oz (1lb)
750g	24oz (1½lb)
1kg	32oz (2lb)

LIQUID MEASURES

Metric	Imperial
30ml	1 fluid oz
60ml	2 fluid oz
100ml	3 fluid oz
125ml	4 fluid oz
150ml	5 fluid oz (¼ pint/1 gill)
190ml	6 fluid oz
250ml	8 fluid oz
300ml	10 fluid oz (½ pint)
500ml	16 fluid oz
600ml	20 fluid oz (1 pint)
1000ml (1 litre)	1¾ pints

HELPFUL MEASURES

Metric	Imperial
3mm	⅛in
6mm	¼in
1cm	½in
2cm	¾in
2.5cm	1in
5cm	2in
6cm	2½in
8cm	3in
10cm	4in
13cm	5in
15cm	6in
18cm	7in
20cm	8in
23cm	9in
25cm	10in
28cm	11in
30cm	12in (1ft)

MEASURING EQUIPMENT

The difference between one country's measuring cups and another's is, at most, within a 2 or 3 teaspoon variance. (For the record, 1 Australian metric measuring cup holds approximately 250ml.) The most accurate way of measuring dry ingredients is to weigh them. When measuring liquids, use a clear glass or plastic jug with the metric markings.

Note: North America and UK use 15ml tablespoons. Australian tablespoons measure 20ml. All cup and spoon measurements are level.

HOW TO MEASURE

When using graduated metric measuring cups, shake dry ingredients loosely into the appropriate cup. Do not tap the cup on a bench or tightly pack the ingredients unless directed to do so. Level top of measuring cups and measuring spoons with a knife. When measuring liquids, place a clear glass or plastic jug with metric markings on a flat surface to check accuracy at eye level.

We use large eggs having an average weight of 60g.

OVEN TEMPERATURES

These oven temperatures are only a guide. Always check the manufacturer's manual.

	C°(Celsius)	F°(Fahrenheit)	Gas Mark
Very slow	120	250	1
Slow	150	300	2
Moderately slow	160	325	3
Moderate	180 - 190	350 - 375	4
Moderately hot	200 - 210	400 - 425	5
Hot	220 - 230	450 - 475	6
Very hot	240 - 250	500 - 525	7

Index

A

Afghan Biscuits 2
Almond Macaroons 72
Anzac Biscuits 2
Apple Brown Betty 4
Apple Cake 5
Apple Charlotte 6
Apple Crumble 7
Apple Pie 7
Apple Sponge 8
Apple Strudel 9
Apples, Baked 10
Apricot Sauce 81
Armenian Nutmeg Cake 9

B

Baked Apples 10
Baked Custard 10
Bakewell Tart 10
Banana Fritters 12
Banana Tart, Caramel 23
Bananas, Caramel 23
Baps 12
Berlin Doughnuts 13
BISCUITS AND SLICES
- Afghan Biscuits 2
- Anzac Biscuits 2
- Brandy Snaps 19
- Butterscotch Buttons 21
- Caramel Chocolate Slice 24
- Caramel Corn Flake Chews 25
- Chester Squares 30
- Chocolate Brownies 31
- Chocolate Chip Cookies 32
- Chocolate Peppermint Slice 35
- Easter Biscuits 47
- Flapjacks (British) 51
- Florentines 51
- Garibaldi Slice 53
- Gingerbread Men 55
- Gingernuts 55
- Honey Joys 59
- Honey Jumbles 59
- Kisses 66
- Macaroons, Almond 72
- Macaroons, Coconut 73
- Melting Moments 78
- Monte Carlos 78
- Old English Matrimonials 82
- Peanut Slice 87
- Scottish Shortbread 101
- Sponge Fingers 104

Black Bottom Pie 15
Black Forest Cheesecake 15
Blancmange, Chocolate 31
Boiled Fruit Cake 16
Boiled Pineapple Fruit Cake 17
Bombe Alaska 17
Boston Brown Bread 18
Brandy Snaps 19
Bread and Butter Pudding 20
Bread, Boston Brown 18
Bread Pudding 20
Bread, Soda 103
BREADS AND BUNS
- Baps 12
- Berlin Doughnuts 13
- Boston Brown Bread 18
- Chelsea Buns 27
- Damper 42
- Fairy Bread 48
- Finger Buns 48
- Hot Cross Buns 61
- Lardy Cake 68
- Soda Bread 103
- Stollen 105

Brown Betty, Apple 4
Brownies, Chocolate 31
Butterfly Cakes 48
Butterscotch Curls 21
Butterscotch Buttons 21

C

CAKES
- Apple Cake 5
- Armenian Nutmeg Cake 9
- Boiled Fruit Cake 16
- Boiled Pineapple Fruit Cake 17
- Carrot Cake 25
- Cheesecakes 26
- Cherry Cake 29
- Cinnamon Teacake 36
- Coconut Cake 36
- Date and Walnut Rolls 43
- Devil's Food Cake 44
- Dundee Cake 46
- Fairy Cakes 48
- Ginger Sponge 57
- Gingerbread 54
- Honey Roll 60
- Hummingbird Cake 62
- Jelly Cakes 64
- Lamingtons 66
- Lumberjack Cake 72
- Madeira Cake 74
- Marble Cake 74
- Napoleon Cake 80
- Orange Cake 82
- Pound Cake 89
- Rainbow Cake 92
- Rich Fruit Cake 94
- Rock Cakes 95
- Sand Cake 98
- Seed Cake, Caraway 101
- Seed Cake, Poppy 101
- Streusel Coffee Cake 106
- Sultana Cake 107
- Swiss Roll 109
- Tipsy Cake 112
- Twelfth Night Cake 116
- Victoria Sandwich 118

Caramel Banana Tart 23
Caramel Bananas 23
Caramel Chocolate Slice 24
Caramel Corn Flake Chews 25
Caramel Sauce 120
Caraway Seed Cake 101
Carrot Cake 25
Chantilly Cream 33, 39
Cheesecake 26
Cheesecake, Black Forest 15
Cheesecake, Lemon 68
Cheesecakes 26
Chelsea Buns 27
Cherries Jubilee 28
Cherry Cake 29
Chester Squares 30
Chocolate Blancmange 31
Chocolate Brownies 31
Chocolate Chip Cookies 32
Chocolate Crackles 32
Chocolate Eclairs 33
Chocolate Mousse 34
Chocolate Peppermint Slice 35
Chocolate Self-Saucing Pudding 35
Chocolate Slice, Caramel 24
Cinnamon Teacake 36
Coconut Cake 36
Coconut Ice 37
Coconut Macaroons 73
Coffee Cake, Streusel 106
College Pudding 38
CONFECTIONERY
- Chocolate Crackles 32
- Coconut Ice 37
- Rocky Road 95
- Rum Balls 96
- Russian Caramels 97
- Toffee Apples 112
- White Christmas 120

Corn Flake Chews, Caramel 25
Cream, Chantilly 33, 39
Cream Horns 39
Cream, Mock 80
Cream Puffs 33
Cream, Vienna 79
Cream, Washed Mock 60
Creamed Rice 39
Creme Anglaise 112
Crepes Suzette 41
Crumble, Apple 7
Custard, Baked 10
Custard, Rice 93
Custard, Tapioca 111
Custard Tart 41

D

Damper 42
Date and Walnut Rolls 43
Date Pudding 44
Date Scones 99
DESSERTS
- Apple Brown Betty 4
- Apple Charlotte 6
- Apple Crumble 7
- Apple Pie 7
- Apple Sponge 8
- Apple Strudel 9
- Baked Apples 10
- Baked Custard 10
- Bakewell Tart 10
- Banana Fritters 12
- Black Bottom Pie 15
- Black Forest Cheesecake 15
- Bombe Alaska 17
- Bread and Butter Pudding 20
- Bread Pudding 20
- Caramel Banana Tart 23
- Caramel Bananas 23
- Cheesecake 26
- Cherries Jubilee 28
- Chocolate Blancmange 31
- Chocolate Mousse 34
- Chocolate Self-Saucing Pudding 35
- College Pudding 38
- Creamed Rice 39
- Crepes Suzette 41
- Custard Tart 41
- Date Pudding 44
- Diplomat Pudding 45
- Ginger Pudding 57
- Golden Syrup Dumplings 58
- Impossible Pie 63
- Key Lime Pie 64
- Lemon Cheesecake 68
- Lemon Chiffon Pie 69
- Lemon Delicious 71
- Lemon Meringue Pie 71
- Marshmallow Pavlova 77
- Nesselrode Ice-Cream 81
- Passionfruit Flummery 84
- Peach Melba 85
- Pecan Pie 87
- Plum Pudding with Hard Sauce 88
- Pumpkin Pie 90
- Queen of Puddings 91
- Rice Custard 93
- Rice Pudding 93
- Rum Baba 96
- Sago Steamed Pudding 98
- Snow Eggs 102
- Spanish Cream 104
- Strawberries Romanoff 106
- Strawberry Shortcake 106
- Summer Pudding 108
- Syllabub 110

Tapioca Custard 111
Tortoni 113
Treacle Tart 114
Trifle 114
Vanilla Ice-Cream 117
Waffles with Caramel Sauce 120
Zabaglione 122
Devil's Food Cake... 44
Diplomat Pudding 45
Doughnuts, Berlin 13
Dumplings, Golden Syrup 58
Dundee Cake 46

E

Easter Biscuits 47
Eccles Cakes 47
Eclairs, Chocolate 33

F

Fairy Bread 48
Fairy Cakes 48
Finger Buns 48
Flapjacks (American)... 51
Flapjacks (British) 51
Floating Islands 102
Florentines 51
Fluffy Frosting 92
Flummery, Passionfruit 84
Fritters, Banana 12
Fruit Cake, Boiled 16
Fruit Cake, Boiled Pineapple 17
Fruit Cake, Rich 94
Fruit Mince Pies 52

G

Garibaldi Slice 53
Gem Scones 54
Ginger Pudding 57
Ginger Sponge 57
Gingerbread 54
Gingerbread Men 55
Gingernuts 55
Golden Syrup Dumplings 58

H

Hard Sauce 88
Honey Joys 59
Honey Jumbles 59
Honey Roll 60
Hot Cross Buns 61
Hummingbird Cake 62

I

Ice-Cream, Nesselrode 81
Ice-Cream, Vanilla 117
ICINGS AND FROSTINGS
    Chocolate Frosting, Rich.................................... 44
    Chocolate Icing 2, 31, 77
    Cream Cheese Frosting 25, 62
    Fluffy Frosting 92
    Glace Icing 80
    Lemon Icing 10, 54, 77
    Orange Icing 83
    Passionfruit Icing 6, 80, 118
    Royal Icing 55
Impossible Pie 63

J

Jelly Cakes... 64

K

Key Lime Pie 64
Kisses 66

L

Lamingtons 66
Lardy Cake 68
Lemon Cheesecake 68

Lemon Chiffon Pie 69
Lemon Delicious 71
Lemon Meringue Pie 71
Lumberjack Cake 72

M

Macaroons, Almond 72
Macaroons, Coconut 73
Madeira Cake 74
Marble Cake 74
Marshmallow Pavlova 77
Matches 77
Melting Moments 78
Mock Cream 80
Mock Cream, Washed 60
Monte Carlos 78
Mousse, Chocolate 34
Mushrooms 79

N

Napoleon Cake 80
Neenish Tarts 80
Nesselrode Ice-Cream 81
Nutmeg Cake, Armenian 9

O

Old English Matrimonials 82
Orange Cake 82

P

Palmiers 83
Pancakes 84
Passionfruit Flummery 84
PASTRY
    Apple Charlotte 6
    Apple Pie 7
    Apple Strudel 9
    Bakewell Tart 10
    Black Bottom Pie 15
    Caramel Banana Tart 23
    Chocolate Eclairs.. 33
    Cream Horns 39
    Custard Tart 41
    Eccles Cakes 47
    Fruit Mince Pies 52
    Key Lime Pie 64
    Lemon Chiffon Pie 69
    Lemon Meringue Pie 71
    Matches 77
    Mushrooms 79
    Napoleon Cake... 80
    Neenish Tarts 80
    Palmiers 83
    Pecan Pie 87
    Pumpkin Pie 90
    Scottish Black Bun 100
    Treacle Tart 114
    Vanilla Slice 118
    Yorkshire Curd Tarts 121
Pavlova, Marshmallow 77
Peach Melba 85
Peanut Slice 87
Pecan Pie 87
Pikelets 87
Pineapple Fruit Cake, Boiled 17
Plum Pudding with Hard Sauce 88
Poppy Seed Cake 101
Pound Cake 89
Pumpkin Pie 90
Pumpkin Scones 90

Q

Queen of Puddings.. 91

R

Rainbow Cake... 92
Raspberry Sauce 85
Rice, Creamed 39
Rice Custard 93
Rice Pudding 93

Rich Fruit Cake 94
Rock Cakes 95
Rocky Road 95
Royal Icing 55
Rum Baba 96
Rum Balls 96
Russian Caramels 97

S

Sago Steamed Pudding 98
Sand Cake 98
SAUCES 99
    Apricot Sauce... 81
    Caramel Sauce 120
    Hard Sauce 88
    Raspberry Sauce... 85
SCONES
    Butterscotch Curls 21
    Date Scones 99
    Gem Scones 54
    Pumpkin Scones 90
    Wholemeal Scones 99
Scottish Black Bun 100
Scottish Shortbread 101
Seed Cake, Caraway 101
Seed Cake, Poppy 101
Self-Saucing Pudding, Chocolate............................ 35
Shortbread, Scottish 101
Shortcake, Strawberry 106
Snow Eggs 102
Soda Bread 103
Spanish Cream 104
Sponge Fingers 104
Sponge, Apple 8
Stollen 105
Strawberries Romanoff 106
Strawberry Shortcake 106
Streusel Coffee Cake 106
Strudel, Apple 9
Sultana Cake 107
Summer Pudding 108
Swiss Roll 109
Syllabub 110

T

Tapioca Custard 111
Teacake, Cinnamon 36
Tipsy Cake 112
Toffee Apples 112
Tortoni 113
Treacle Tart 114
Trifle.. 114
Twelfth Night Cake 116

V

Vanilla Ice-Cream 117
Vanilla Slice 118
Victoria Sandwich.. 118
Vienna Cream 66, 79

W

Waffles with Caramel Sauce................................. 120
Walnut Rolls, Date and 43
Washed Mock Cream 60
White Christmas 120
Wholemeal Scones 99
Wholemeal Soda Bread 103

Y

Yorkshire Curd Tards 121

Z

Zabaglione 122